CAMPAIGN • 232

THE *BISMARCK* 1941

Hunting Germany's greatest battleship

ANGUS KONSTAM

ILLUSTRATED BY PAUL WRIGHT

Series editor Marcus Cowper

First published in Great Britain in 2011 by Osprey Publishing.
Part of Bloomsbury Publishing Plc. PO Box 883, Oxford, OX1 9PL, UK
1385 Broadway, 5th Floor, New York, NY10018, USA

Email: info@ospreypublishing.com

A CIP catalogue record for this book is available from the British Library.

ISBN: 978 1 84908 383 6 – First published 2011. 4th impression 2015.

eBook ISBN: 978 1 84908 384 3

Editorial by Ilios Publishing Ltd, Oxford, UK (www.iliospublishing.com)
Page layout by The Black Spot
Index by Sandra Shotter
Typeset in Sabon and Myriad Pro
Maps by bounford.com
Bird's-eye views by Ian Palmer
Battlescene illustrations by Paul Wright
Originated by PPS Grasmere Ltd.
Printed and bound by PrintOnDemand-Worldwide.com Peterborough UK

Transferred to digital print on demand 2017

www.ospreypublishing.com

AUTHOR'S NOTE

In this book all ranges and distances are measured in nautical miles.

During World War II gun ranges were measured in yards in the Royal Navy,
and metres in the Kriegsmarine.

Theoretically, a nautical mile varies with latitude, as it represents the
equivalent of one minute of current latitude, which is shorter towards the
poles than it is at the equator. For the sake of simplicity we have adopted
the Royal Naval system throughout, which was – and still is – used for the
calculation of gunnery ranges.

1 nautical mile = 2,000 yards (or 10 cables), or 1,852m. It is the equivalent
of 1.15 land miles.

Unless otherwise indicated all images are part of the author's collection.

ARTIST'S NOTE

Readers may care to note that the original paintings from which the
colour plates in this book were prepared are available for private sale.
The Publishers retain all reproduction copyright whatsoever.
All enquiries should be addressed to:

p.wright1@btinternet.com

The Publishers regret that they can enter into no correspondence upon
this matter.

THE WOODLAND TRUST

Osprey Publishing are supporting the Woodland Trust, the UK's leading
woodland conservation charity, by funding the dedication of trees.

CONTENTS

INTRODUCTION 5

CHRONOLOGY 8

ORIGINS OF THE CAMPAIGN 10

OPPOSING COMMANDERS 15
Royal Navy . Kriegsmarine

OPPOSING FLEETS 19
Royal Navy . Kriegsmarine

OPPOSING PLANS 26
Royal Navy . Kriegsmarine

THE CAMPAIGN 30
The break-out . The battle of the Denmark Strait . The pursuit . The last battle

AFTERMATH 88

THE SHIPWRECK 92

BIBLIOGRAPHY 94

INDEX 95

The North Atlantic, May 1941

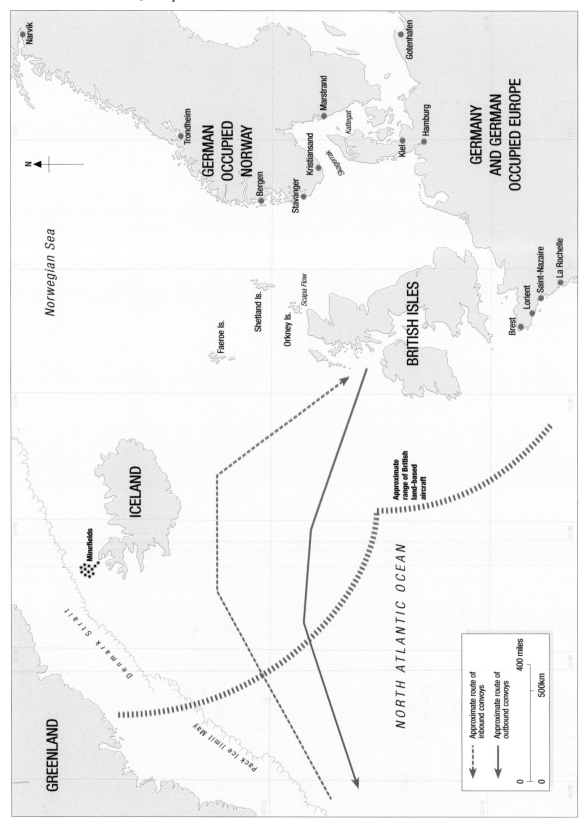

INTRODUCTION

There was no other warship like her. In the spring of 1941, a combination of German steel, an impressive and integrated armament, and an excellent design made the *Bismarck* one of the most powerful warships in the world. The Germans claimed she was unsinkable – the ultimate battleship. This is why she posed such a threat to Britain during those dark months of 1941 – she was a floating challenge to British naval prestige and supremacy, and she might well be as invincible as the German propagandists claimed. She entered service in August 1940, when Britain was still fighting for her life in the Battle of Britain and German invasion barges filled the French channel ports. For nine months the *Bismarck* remained one of the most serious latent threats Britain faced – a warship that could single-handedly sever her vital maritime lifeline and bring the beleaguered island nation to her knees.

In early 1941, Germany's U-boats were causing devastation in the Atlantic, and hundreds of thousands of tons of Allied shipping were being sunk every month. While the Battle of the Atlantic was going well, Großadmiral Erich Raeder was also aware that he still lacked enough U-boats to have a decisive impact. To starve the British of the resources they needed to continue fighting, the commander of the Kriegsmarine (the German Navy) knew that he had to use all the assets at his disposal. That included the *Bismarck*.

The KMS *Bismarck* in happier days, pictured during her 'working-up' exercises in the Baltic Sea, sailing in consort with the *Prinz Eugen*. The chevrons of her 'Baltic camouflage scheme' were painted over during her brief sojourn in Norwegian waters.

HMS *Hood* entering Portsmouth in April 1937 during preparations for the Royal Fleet Review. This elegant old battlecruiser might have been the pride of the Royal Navy, but by 1941 her poor armour meant modern battleships outclassed her.

Given the situation, both sides knew that the *Bismarck* would make a sortie into the Atlantic – her target the convoys whose survival were entwined with that of Britain. That spring, both fleets prepared for the clash. The German battleship had become the new bogeyman for the sailors of the Royal Navy's Home Fleet, based in Scapa Flow. Their commander Vice Admiral John Tovey was prepared to do anything he could to intercept and destroy the *Bismarck* when she made her move. He realized just how high the stakes had become. Not only was the reputation of the Royal Navy at stake, but the *Bismarck* also posed the direst possible threat to Britain's maritime lifeline. Whatever happened, she had to be located, caught and sunk.

The Germans planned to unleash the *Bismarck* in May 1941 – her maiden voyage would be a sortie deep into the North Atlantic, codenamed Operation *Rheinübung*. The *Bismarck* was considered fast enough to slip past the British warships blocking her path into the Atlantic, and, if it came to a fight, her guns were considered more than a match for any single battleship that the Royal Navy could send against her.

The short naval campaign that followed pitted the *Bismarck* against the might of the Royal Navy – a tense drama played out against the cold, grey backdrop of the North Atlantic. Even the most experienced sailor can find the North Atlantic a grim, forbidding place, where storm-tossed grey seas merge with a glowering grey sky to create a harsh, unremitting environment, which isn't conducive to smooth-running naval operations. Looking at a map also gives a false impression of the scale of the campaign. This was a giant maritime game of cat and mouse, only the prey was no docile creature but a powerful modern battleship, with the speed, firepower and armour to fight her way out of trouble if the need arose. Finding a single ship in the vast expanse of the North Atlantic is a difficult task today, but in 1941 it was that much harder as the weather conditions were poor, radar was in its infancy, and, for a crucial 24 hours, the British had no real idea where to look.

The newly built *Bismarck*, pictured as she was being towed out from the outfitting wharf at Hamburg's Blohm & Voss shipyard. This photograph was taken at the start of her initial trials in mid-September 1940, three weeks after she was commissioned.

This would end in one of two ways. One would be that the Royal Navy would destroy the *Bismarck*, thereby restoring the naval status quo, and allowing the Admiralty to concentrate their resources on fighting the menace of the U-boats. German naval confidence would be shattered and her remaining surface warships would be consigned to a defensive role. The other would be that the *Bismarck* would evade her pursuers, cause havoc in the transatlantic shipping lanes and return safely to port, where she could threaten to repeat the sortie whenever she liked. This would be an immense blow to British naval prestige, and call into question Britain's very ability to continue the war. As the *Bismarck* prepared for sea, both sides realized just how important the coming few days would be.

CHRONOLOGY

July 1936	Keel of *Bismarck* laid in Hamburg.
February 1939	*Bismarck* launched.
August 1940	*Bismarck* commissioned into the Kriegsmarine.
Sept–Nov 1940	The *Bismarck* conducts sea trials in the Baltic Sea.
December 1940	She returns to Hamburg for final outfitting.

1941

March	Sails from Hamburg to Gotenhafen (Gdynia) on the Baltic.
April	Final sea trials and crew training exercises.
5 May	Hitler inspects the *Bismarck*, accompanied by Admiral Lütjens.
12 May	Admiral Lütjens and staff embark.

Sunday 18 May

| | Start of Operation *Rheinübung*. |
| *12pm* | *Bismarck* slips her berth and anchors in Gotenhafen Bay to take on fuel and last-minute supplies. |

Monday 19 May

2am	*Bismarck* proceeds to sea, accompanied by the *Prinz Eugen*.
12pm	Rendezvous with two destroyers off island of Rügen.
11.30pm	German Seekampfgruppe (naval task force) joined by a third destroyer.

Tuesday 20 May

| *2am* | Seekampfgruppe begins four hour transit of the Great Belt in Danish waters. |
| *1pm* | *Bismarck* sighted in the Kattegat by the Swedish cruiser *Gotland*. |

Wednesday 21 May

8am	Seekampfgruppe enters the Korsfjord, near Bergen.
11am	*Bismarck* anchors in the Grimstadfjord, an arm of the Korsfjord.
1.15pm	*Bismarck* spotted by Coastal Command Reconnaissance Plane.
8pm	Seekampfgruppe departs from the Korsfjord, and proceeds to sea, heading north.

Thursday 22 May

12.15am	Holland sails from Scapa Flow with *Hood* and *Prince of Wales*.
2am	Bombing attack on the Grimstadfjord.
4.20am	The German destroyers are detached, and return to the Korsfjord.
12pm	*Bismarck* and *Prinz Eugen* in Norwegian Sea, still heading north at 24 knots.
1.10pm	Course altered towards the Denmark Strait.
9pm	Tovey learns that the *Bismarck* has sailed from Grimstadfjord.
11pm	Tovey sails from Scapa with *King George V* and *Victorious*.

Friday 23 May

6pm	Seekampfgruppe approaches Denmark Strait, reaches limit of pack ice. Course altered to the south-west.
7.22pm	Suffolk sights *Bismarck*, and reports her position.
8.30pm	*Bismarck* sights *Norfolk*, and engages her, without scoring a hit. Forward radar damaged by the blast. *Prinz Eugen* takes the lead.
10pm	British cruisers evade the *Bismarck*, and shadow her through the night.

Saturday 24 May

	Battle of the Denmark Strait.
5.37am	German Seekampfgruppe sights *Hood* and *Prince of Wales* at range of 17 miles (31km).
5.52am	British ships open fire, *Hood* targeting *Prinz Eugen*, and *Prince of Wales* firing at *Bismarck*.
5.54am	*Prinz Eugen* opens fire on *Hood*.
5.55am	*Bismarck* opens fire on *Hood*.
6am	*Hood* hit by salvo from *Bismarck* and blows up.
6.02am	*Bismarck* switches fire to *Prince of Wales*, quickly scores hits. *Prince of Wales* also scores at least one hit on *Bismarck*.
6.05am	*Prince of Wales* retires from the battle.
6.09am	*Bismarck* ceases fire. Damage control report oil leak.
12.40pm	Lütjens heads south, still shadowed by British cruisers.
6.15pm	*Prinz Eugen* detached, leaving *Bismarck* to continue on alone. Owing to fuel leak Lütjens decides to put in to Saint-Nazaire.

Sunday 25 May

12.15am	*Bismarck* attacked by Swordfish from *Victorious*; one torpedo hit amidships, but no significant damage caused.
1.31am	*Bismarck* engages *Prince of Wales*, but no hits are inflicted.
3.15am	*Bismarck* alters course and evades pursuers.
9.30am	Lütjens radios Germany, giving detailed report. The signal is intercepted.

Monday 26 May

10.30am	*Bismarck* spotted by Catalina flying boat.
5.40pm	Sheffield locates and shadows *Bismarck*.
9pm	*Bismarck* attacked by Swordfish from *Ark Royal*. Hit twice, and rudder jammed.
9.30pm	*Bismarck* fires on Sheffield, but no hits inflicted.
9.40pm	Lütjens radios Germany, reporting *Bismarck* can no longer manoeuvre.
10.40pm	*Bismarck* shadowed by Polish destroyer *Piorun* and three British destroyers.
11.59pm	Lütjens radios Germany, reporting hopeless situation. Speed now 7 knots.

Tuesday 27 May

7.10am	Lütjens sends final signal.
8.45am	*Bismarck* sighted by *Rodney* and *King George V*.
8.47am	*Rodney* opens fire. followed a minute later by *King George V*.
8.49am	*Bismarck* returns fire.
8.59am	*Bismarck* receives first 16in. hit from *Rodney*. Main gunnery director destroyed.
9.02am	Forward turrets knocked out, after gunnery director put out of action.
9.27am	Dora turret knocked out, fires raging.
9.30am	Caesar turret knocked out – *Bismarck*'s guns now silenced.
10.24am	Hit by two torpedoes from *Dorsetshire*, followed by a second salvo six minutes later.
10.40am	*Bismarck* finally sinks. 116 survivors recovered from the water.

ORIGINS OF THE CAMPAIGN

For the Royal Navy, the showdown with the *Bismarck* could hardly have come at a worse time. The 'Senior Service' was stretched to its limit, fighting a bitter two-front naval war in both the Atlantic Ocean and the Mediterranean. The 'phoney war' ended in the early summer of 1940 when the whirlwind German invasion of France that May was followed in June by Italy entering the war as Germany's ally. Britain's resources were now committed, as the peacetime navy lacked the ships and men it needed to guarantee victory in both spheres of operation.

That summer the British Mediterranean Fleet was immediately pitched into a vicious naval campaign for supremacy, and by the spring of 1941 it appeared to have gained the upper hand. Victories at Taranto and Cape Matapan deprived the Italian Supermarina of some of its most powerful warships, and its commanders became increasingly reluctant to risk the rest of their fleet in a battle they felt they couldn't win.

The battleship *Bismarck*, photographed shortly after she was commissioned into service. Before undertaking Operation *Rheinübung*, she underwent a considerable crew training and 'working-up' programme in the relative safety of the Baltic Sea, before being declared ready for operational duty in April 1941.

Then in April, less than a month before the *Bismarck* slipped out to sea, everything changed. Germany invaded Yugoslavia and Greece, and within weeks the Royal Navy was called in to evacuate Commonwealth and Greek soldiers, first from Greece and then from Crete. The Germans had moved hundreds of aircraft to the region, and warships began to be bombed and sunk in ever-increasing numbers. When Churchill suggested withdrawing the fleet, Cunningham replied; 'it takes three years to build a ship. It takes three centuries to build a tradition'. The evacuation continued. The losses ended

after the final evacuation of Crete, but the incident taxed the resources of the Royal Navy even further, as replacements from the Home Fleet had to be sent to the Mediterranean to help make up for the losses. The Royal Navy was now stretched very thinly indeed.

The past 12 months had also seen a dramatic change in home waters. In April 1940 the Germans invaded Norway, which gave them control of Norway's airfields and numerous secluded anchorages. The collapse of France in May and June 1940 meant that the Germans now controlled France's Atlantic ports, the most important of which were Brest, Cherbourg and Saint-Nazaire. The first arm of the Kriegsmarine to use them was the U-boat fleet, but ports were also perfectly suited as bases for Germany's major surface warships. The occupation of the Channel ports also raised the possibility of a German invasion of Britain. While the Luftwaffe vied for control of the skies, German troops prepared for a cross-channel invasion, and landing barges were gathered in the French Channel ports.

Since the war began the Kriegsmarine had been waging a U-boat campaign against Britain. As early as August 1939 the Kriegsmarine's Seekriegsleitung (operations department) ordered its U-boat forces to engage in 'commerce warfare' – in other words to attack British shipping. Starved of fuel for her ships and aircraft, food for her population or steel for her ships, Britain would be brought to her knees. If her maritime links overseas were severed, Britain would be unable to wage war, or defend her global possessions, In World War I, German U-boats had almost succeeded in severing Britain's maritime arteries. The Kriegsmarine's Commander-in-Chief Großadmiral Raeder was determined that this time Germany would succeed.

This enterprise – an operation that evolved into the Battle of the Atlantic – would be spearheaded by the Kriegsmarine's U-boat arm. However, Raeder also saw a role for his major surface warships. When the war broke out the Kriegsmarine sent the pocket battleship *Graf Spee* on a rampage through the South Atlantic and the Indian Ocean – a spree that lasted for ten weeks before a squadron of British cruisers caught up with her off the River Plate, damaging her enough for the German warship to flee into a neutral port. She put to sea again only to scuttle herself off Montevideo, her captain preferring to save lives rather than make his crew face a battle against overwhelming odds.

Then in January 1941 the battlecruisers *Scharnhorst* and *Gneisenau* broke out into the North Atlantic, where they sank 22 merchant ships, totalling some 115,000 tons. This sortie – codenamed Operation *Berlin* – was a complete success. The two battlecruisers passed through the Denmark Strait between Greenland and Iceland, then spent two months disrupting Allied convoys in the mid-Atlantic before returning safely to Brest in late March. The force was commanded by Admiral Lütjens, the man chosen to lead the *Bismarck* and *Prinz Eugen* on a similar sortie less than two months after his triumphal return.

Apart from the loss of the *Graf Spee*, these sorties had been successful, and made the Seekriegsleitung believe that further operations of this kind were a useful way to increase the pressure on the British, whose transatlantic lifeline was already under pressure from the U-boats. If such impressive results could be achieved with battlecruisers, even greater success could be expected if the far more powerful *Bismarck* managed to break out into the North Atlantic. Therefore, within a fortnight of Lütjens' safe arrival in Brest, plans were being drawn up for a new operation.

On 2 April, just 11 days after Lütjens' homecoming, Generaladmiral Otto Schniewind, Chief of Staff of the Seekriegsleitung, issued a new directive, which had just been approved by Großadmiral Raeder. It emphasized the strategic importance of these surface ship sorties into the Atlantic, and outlined what their objectives were. In effect it laid out the reasons behind the German strategy and showed what Raeder hoped to achieve. From this, it was clear that the *Bismarck*, which was conducting her final sea trials in the Baltic Sea, would spearhead the next sortie.

The elegant battlecruiser HMS *Hood*, photographed at anchor in Scapa Flow. She was built during World War I, but inter-war parsimony meant that she was never fully modernized, and she lacked the armoured protection of more modern major warships.

This aggressive use of his major surface ships was typical of Raeder. During World War I the Commander-in-Chief of the Kriegsmarine had been Chief of Staff to Admiral Hipper, who commanded the German battlecruisers at the battle of Jutland (1916). After Jutland the German Hochseeflotte (High Seas Fleet) spent the rest of the war on the defensive and its ships rarely left port. Raeder was determined to use his capital ships more aggressively than his predecessors.

Adolf Hitler, posing for photographers during his inspection of the *Bismarck* and *Prinz Eugen* in Gotenhafen on 1 May 1941. He never grasped the importance of seapower, and had reservations about the value of capital ships.

In April, Admiral Lütjens was called to Berlin to discuss the possibility of another sortie with Raeder and Schniewind. After Raeder gave his approval, Schniewind and Lütjens planned this new operation, which was given the code name of Operation *Rheinübung* (*Rhine Exercise*). When plans were first drafted Schniewind and Lütjens expected to have a powerful Seekampfgruppe at their disposal – the battleship *Bismarck*, the two battlecruisers, *Scharnhorst* and *Gneisenau*, and the heavy cruiser *Prinz Eugen*. German destroyers lacked the fuel capacity and endurance to operate in the North Atlantic. German aircraft also lacked the range to provide cover. Only the U-boat fleet was in a position to provide the Seekampfgruppe with support – acting as scouts, and helping to track enemy convoys. Apart from them, these large and powerful German surface ships would be left to their own devices.

The trouble was, the *Scharnhorst* and the *Gneisenau* were still in Brest on the French Atlantic coast, while the *Bismarck* and the *Prinz Eugen* were half a continent away, in the Baltic Sea. The original plan was for the two groups to rendezvous in mid-Atlantic, after the German ships had successfully evaded the waiting British warships. Obviously this operation was an extremely risky venture. Not only did it place all of Germany's capital ships in danger, but they would venture into hostile waters, beyond the reach of any help if anything went wrong.

While the British Home Fleet was stretched thin, it still had enough battleships to crush either of the two Seekampfgruppen if they could bring them to battle. Of course, if the two German Seekampfgruppen managed to join forces, the whole situation would be very different. They would then have the firepower to take on the British Home Fleet, and they had the speed to dictate whether they would fight, or evade contact, only to fall on some unprotected convoy instead. While Schniewind and Lütjens realized that any attempt to wrest control of the Atlantic Ocean from the Royal Navy was pure fantasy, they knew they had a chance of inflicting a humiliating defeat on the British, and of disrupting or even halting Britain's vital transatlantic convoys. This would be the biggest, most ambitious German naval operation of the war.

While Raeder encouraged the aggressive use of his major ships, he realized that if any of his warships were damaged in mid-Atlantic, then their chances of reaching a friendly port were extremely limited. Consequently, Lütjens – the man chosen to lead the operation – was ordered to preserve his ships as best he could, engaging enemy warships only when an encounter was unavoidable. His priority was to destroy enemy convoys, not to lock horns with Royal Naval battleships. When he approved the operation, Raeder added another cautionary note, 'It would be a mistake to risk a heavy engagement for limited and perhaps uncertain results'.

It was a strategy of limited risk – one that left Lütjens in the difficult position of having to decide whether to avoid a fight, or to press home an advantage against the enemy if events presented him with an opportunity. In the end, this is exactly the situation he found himself in on 24 May. There his options were simply to fight the enemy, or to slink back to a home port having failed in his mission. For an aggressive commander like Lütjens there was simply no question what he should do.

Then, on 6 April 1941, the whole situation changed. While they lay docked in Brest the German battlecruisers were the target of a major bombing raid by the Royal Air Force. A Beaufort torpedo bomber managed to fly through the curtain of flak, and, although the aircraft was hit, her crew managed to drop their torpedo before the plane crashed. The torpedo struck the *Gneisenau*, causing moderate damage. Four nights later the RAF struck again, and this time five bombs struck the battlecruiser. The result of these two raids was that the *Gneisenau* was put out of action, and needed to be dry-docked and repaired, a process that could take several months.

The *Scharnhorst* was also undergoing a refit that was expected to last for up to two months. While this could be cut short, her chances of successfully breaking out into the Atlantic on her own were significantly less than if she could operate in consort with her sister ship. It was decided to continue with the refit, and hope that the *Gneisenau* could be repaired as quickly as possible.

That left the Baltic Seekampfgruppe – *Bismarck* and *Prinz Eugen*. The original plan called for the two ships to commence Operation *Rheinübung* on 28 April. However, the *Prinz Eugen* was slightly damaged by a magnetic mine, dropped by a British aircraft, and so the sortie was postponed for almost four weeks while repairs were carried out. Therefore, Admiral Lütjens set a new starting date in late May, to take advantage of a new moon and the consequent reduction in visibility this entailed. The dark nights made it easier to slip past through the cordon of British ships. Actually, Lütjens had wanted to delay the operation even further, which would allow him to add the *Bismarck*'s sister ship *Tirpitz* to his Seekampfgruppe. That May the *Tirpitz* was conducting sea trials and would be ready for active service by the end of June. That would have placed an extremely powerful force at his disposal. Unfortunately for Lütjens, Raeder refused to countenance any further delay. Lütjens would simply have to make the most of the *Bismarck* and the *Prinz Eugen*. The scene was now set for one of the deadliest and most tragic naval operations of World War II.

OPPOSING COMMANDERS

Vice Admiral John Tovey (1885–1971), the commander of the Home Fleet based in Scapa Flow was a confident and professional commander, although his stubbornness earned him the dislike of Winston Churchill. Tovey orchestrated the hunt of the *Bismarck* with commendable skill.

ROYAL NAVY

Admiral Sir Dudley Pound (1877–1943)

The First Sea Lord and Chief of Naval Staff, Sir Dudley was the man responsible for guiding British naval strategy. In effect he had complete operational, administrative and political control of the wartime Royal Navy. He was based in the Admiralty in London, although he also held an important advisory post to the War Cabinet, which in turn advised the Prime Minister Sir Winston Churchill. Pound therefore bore a heavy responsibility, but he was ably assisted by the rest of the Admiralty, whose various departments provided the Navy with logistical and administrative support, oversaw new ship construction and the readiness of the fleet. While Pound had his advisers, he alone bore the responsibility for operational decision-making.

He became First Sea Lord in July 1939, and for the next two years he managed to prevent excessive interference in naval affairs by Churchill or the War Cabinet. He had a distinguished career. He commanded the dreadnought battleship HMS *Colossus* at Jutland (1916), and between the wars he commanded the Mediterranean Fleet. He proved an efficient First Sea Lord, but by early 1941 he was suffering from the brain tumour that finally killed him two-and-a-half years later. He was the man responsible for formulating Britain's response to the German U-boat threat, and, while he was criticized for certain decisions – most notably his order to Convoy PQ-17 telling it to scatter – he was a reliable and conscientious Commander-in-Chief. One of his innovations was to have a direct telephone link established between his office in the Admiralty and the flagship of the Commander-in-Chief of the Home Fleet, based in Scapa Flow. Attached to a buoy, as long as the flagship was in Scapa Flow, the phone link allowed him to discuss plans directly with the man whose job it was to intercept and destroy the *Bismarck*.

Vice Admiral Sir John Tovey (1885–1971)

Commander-in-Chief of the Home Fleet John Tovey joined the Royal Navy in 1900, and at Jutland (1916) he commanded the destroyer HMS *Onslow*, which played a leading role in the sinking of the German light cruiser *Wiesbaden*, an incident that earned him the Distinguished Service Order (DSO). Between the wars he commanded the battleship HMS *Rodney*, and became the second-in-command of the Mediterranean Fleet. However, he always saw himself as a 'destroyer man'. He became commander of the Home

Fleet in November 1940. By early 1941 Tovey was 56 years old, but he looked much younger. He was deeply religious, with a strong sense of morality and justice. It was said he was hard working and exuded professional competence. Superiors and contemporaries also described him as obstinate, with a sense of purpose that brooked no questions from others. That said, he was a dignified, gentlemanly commander who cared for the welfare of all those in the Senior Service, regardless of rank or station. He also had a poor relationship with both the Prime Minister and the First Sea Lord, and this played a part in his transfer in the summer of 1943, a move which was sweetened by promotion to Admiral of the Fleet.

The main job of the Home Fleet was to prevent any sortie by German surface warships into the Atlantic. During the pursuit of the *Bismarck* he displayed tenacity and resolve, and his leadership during the high-speed chase across the North Atlantic helped bring about the defeat of his quarry. He had already led the chase of the *Scharnhorst* and *Gneisenau*, and let them elude him. This time he had no intention of letting the *Bismarck* slip through his fingers.

Vice Admiral Lancelot Holland (1887–1941)

Holland commanded the Home Fleet's Battlecruiser Squadron, a title that really meant that he was Tovey's second in command. Shortly before the war he served in the Admiralty as Assistant Chief of Naval Staff and at the Air Ministry before being selected for operational command in 1940. He became a rear admiral in 1938, and was promoted to vice admiral two years later. Holland had an active wartime career, having commanded a cruiser squadron in the Mediterranean, which he handled with distinction at the battle of Cape Spartivento (1940). In May 1941 he was sent to Scapa Flow as Vice Admiral Tovey's deputy, and he hoisted his flag in HMS *Hood* just four days before the *Bismarck* sailed.

Vice Admiral Sir James Somerville (1882–1949)

The commander of Force H joined the Royal Navy as a naval cadet in 1897, and during World War I he took part in the Gallipoli operation, where he won the DSO. He became a rear admiral in 1933, and commanded light forces in the Mediterranean, before being invalided out of the service with suspected tuberculosis. This proved to be a false alarm, and he returned to active service, taking command of Force H in the summer of 1940. It was his warships that bombarded the French at Mers-el-Kebir, a regrettable but necessary act of war. Somerville was energetic, fun-loving and straightforward, with a lively personality. While he was never viewed as a cerebral commander, his aggressive spirit earned him a reputation as a 'fighting admiral', and he knew how to inspire his subordinates with his sense of energy and zeal.

Rear Admiral William Wake-Walker (1888–1945)

Wake-Walker was a specialist in torpedo warfare, and, having spent most of the inter-war years in cruisers, he was widely regarded as the most gifted commander of scouting forces in the Royal Navy – a man who could be relied upon to locate an enemy, and to keep shadowing him come what may. He entered the Navy in 1908, was appointed to the rank of rear admiral in September 1939, and commander of the 12th Cruiser Squadron. He played a leading part in organizing the evacuation of troops from Dunkirk, and in January 1941 he took command of the 1st Cruiser Squadron, based in Scapa Flow. A humourless but professional and intuitive commander, he was a good friend of Vice Admiral Tovey, who relied on him to locate and shadow the *Bismarck* when she tried to break out into the Atlantic.

Admiral Günther Lütjens (1889–1941) was one of the most able senior officers in the Kriegsmarine. In 1940 he led the battlecruisers *Scharnhorst* and *Gneisenau* on a highly successful sortie into the Atlantic. He expected Operation *Rheinübung* would achieve even greater results.

KRIEGSMARINE

Großadmiral Erich Raeder (1876–1960)

The Oberbefehlshaber (Ob.d.M.) or Supreme Commander of the Kriegsmarine, Raeder was the real architect of Operation *Rheinübung*. The son of a teacher from Wandsbek in Schleswig-Holstrein, Raeder joined the Kriegsmarine in 1894, and was eventually appointed as the Chief of Staff to Admiral Hipper, the commander of Germany's battlecruisers.

He saw action at Jutland (1916), and remained in the Kriegsmarine after the war, becoming its head in 1928. As Oberbefehlshaber he oversaw the development of the U-boat building programme, and the creation of a powerful surface. A thoroughly efficient staff assisted him. His Berlin-based headquarters also housed the Seekriegsleitung, headed by the gifted Generaladmiral Otto Schniewind. He was assisted by Admiral Kurt Fricke, Operationsabteilungleiter, and Vizeadmiral Hubert Schmundt, the Befehlshaber der Kreuzer (Commander-in-Chief of Cruisers), a post that effectively made him commander of the surface fleet.

Raeder followed the course of the operation closely, but in theory he also had to deal with a chain of command that involved two intermediary links. While operating in Norwegian waters – anywhere outside the Baltic and to the east of Iceland – the *Bismarck* and *Prinz Eugen* would come under the command of Generaladmiral Rolf Carls, the commander of Gruppe Nord, which was based in Wilhelmshaven. Once the ships reached the Atlantic they would technically be controlled by Generaladmiral Alfred Saalwächter, the commander of Gruppe West, based in Berlin. In practical terms, however, Admiral Lütjens and his command was too important to the Kriegsmarine to allow the chain of command to get in the way of operations. Consequently, Lütjens took his orders directly from Raeder, and the two *Gruppen* commanders were ordered to do what they could to support him.

Raeder never convinced Hitler of the need for a powerful navy, and after Operation *Rheinübung* the dictator became increasingly disillusioned with both Raeder and the Kriegsmarine. He was replaced as Oberbefehlshaber in early 1943. Imprisoned after the war, he was released in 1955 and died five years later.

Kapitän zur See Ernst Lindemann (1894–1941) commanded the *Bismarck* during Operation *Rheinübung*. An expert in naval gunnery, he took command of the battleship in 1939, and worked hard to make *Bismarck* an efficient warship. He was still on board when she sank.

Kapitän zur See Helmuth Brinkmann (1895–1983) who commanded the *Prinz Eugen* was a former classmate of Lindemann, and the two captains were on friendly terms. During Operation *Rheinübung* Brinkmann proved himself to be a resourceful commander, evading the British to reach safety.

Admiral Günther Lütjens (1889–1941)

Lütjens was one of the most able operational commanders in the Kriegsmarine. Born in Wiesbaden, he entered the navy in 1907, and served in torpedo boats during World War I. His first major command was the light cruiser *Karlsrühe* in 1934, and the following year he was appointed to the staff of Gruppe Nord. He then served in various staff posts before becoming Führer der Torpedoboote (Flag Officer, Torpedo Boats) in 1937. When the war began he became Befehlshaber der Aufklärungsstreitkräfte (Commander, Scouting Forces), which gave him valuable operational experience.

In April 1940 Lütjens flew his flag in the battlecruiser *Gneisenau*, and saw action off Norway during a brief engagement with the British battlecruiser *Renown*. He was awarded the Knight's Cross for his performance during the Norwegian campaign. In September 1940 Lütjens became an Admiral, and the following January led the *Scharnhorst* and *Gneisenau* on their Atlantic sortie – Operation *Berlin*. He was the perfect choice for a Seekampfgruppe commander, and the man who would put Operation *Rheinübung* into action. He was a thoughtful, reserved commander, and could be relied upon to weigh all the options before gambling with the lives of his men. Despite later claims, he was no admirer of the Nazis and insisted on giving Hitler a proper naval salute when he inspected the *Bismarck* shortly before she sailed.

Kapitän zur See Ernst Lindemann (1894–1941)

The commander of Germany's most modern battleship was a 45-year-old gunnery expert from the Rhineland, who first saw active service during World War I. He rose through the ranks during the inter-war years, and in 1938 was promoted to *Kapitän zur See* and given command of the *Bismarck* when she was commissioned two years later.

Lindemann chain-smoked cigarettes and drank coffee all the time, which may explain why he was seen as a man of boundless energy. According to *Bismarck* survivors he disagreed with Lütjens over the decision to break off action with the *Prince of Wales* after the battle of the Denmark Strait, which indicates an aggressive spirit, but one based on a sound appreciation of the fighting qualities of his ship and its crew. He went down with his ship, and was posthumously awarded the Knight's Cross.

Kapitän zur See Helmuth Brinkmann (1895–1983)

The captain of the *Prinz Eugen* was a native of Lübeck, and a former classmate of Kapitän Lindemann. He saw extensive active service during World War I, and was given his first command in the 1920s. This was followed by various staff appointments that lasted until August 1940, when he was given command of the *Prinz Eugen*. During Operation *Rheinübung* Brinkmann handled the *Prinz Eugen* with commendable skill, and, unlike Lütjens, he managed to bring his ship and his men safely back to port. He was promoted to flag rank shortly after his return and spent the remainder of the war commanding naval forces in the Baltic and Black seas, doing what he could to support German land operations against the Soviet Union.

OPPOSING FLEETS

ROYAL NAVY

Vice Admiral Tovey, Commander-in-Chief of the Home Fleet flew his flag in the brand-new battleship HMS *King George V*, which rode at anchor in Scapa Flow. She was one of four capital ships in the great fleet anchorage, the others being her sister ship HMS *Prince of Wales*, the venerable battlecruiser HMS *Hood* and the Illustrious-class aircraft carrier HMS *Victorious*. The battlecruiser HMS *Repulse* was in the Firth of Clyde, where she was preparing to escort a convoy to Egypt. *Victorious* was due to join her in a few days, and her decks were already filled with Hurricane fighters destined for Malta. Two other capital ships – the powerful HMS *Rodney* and the obsolete Royal Sovereign-class battleship HMS *Ramillies* were busy escorting transatlantic convoys. HMS *Revenge*, another Royal Sovereign class, was in Halifax, Nova Scotia. Tovey also had two heavy cruisers under his command – HMS *Norfolk* and HMS *Suffolk* – which were already patrolling the Denmark Straits, plus several light cruisers and destroyers.

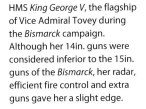

HMS *King George V*, the flagship of Vice Admiral Tovey during the *Bismarck* campaign. Although her 14in. guns were considered inferior to the 15in. guns of the *Bismarck*, her radar, efficient fire control and extra guns gave her a slight edge.

He could also call upon other naval commands for help, the most important of which was Vice Admiral Somerville's Force H, based at Gibraltar, whose core was the aircraft carrier HMS *Ark Royal*, the battlecruiser HMS *Renown* (Somerville's flagship) and the light cruiser HMS *Sheffield*. The light cruiser

HMS *Dorsetshire* was in the South Atlantic, while Plymouth Command included Captain Vian's flotilla of destroyers: HMS *Cossack*, HMS *Maori*, HMS *Sikh*, HMS *Zulu* and the Polish destroyer *Piorun*.

The Home Fleet, 21 May 1941

In Scapa Flow

Battleships (2): *King George V* (Flagship of Vice Admiral Tovey), *Prince of Wales*

Battlecruisers (1): *Hood* (Flagship of Vice Admiral Holland)

Aircraft carriers (1): *Victorious*

Light cruisers (4): *Galatea* (Flagship of Rear Admiral Curteis), *Aurora, Kenya, Neptune*

Destroyers (11): *Achates, Active, Antelope, Anthony, Echo, Electra, Icarus, Inglefield, Intrepid, Nestor, Punjabi*

At sea or on detached duty

Battlecruiser: *Repulse*

Heavy cruisers (2): *Norfolk* (Flagship of Rear Admiral Wake-Walker), *Suffolk*

Light cruisers (5): *Arethusa, Birmingham, Edinburgh, Hermione, Manchester*

Destroyers (5): *Eskimo, Jupiter, Mashona, Somali, Tartar*

While the Home Fleet looked powerful enough, Tovey was well aware that it had its weaknesses. For a start, while his flagship *King George V* had been in service for six months, her sister ship *Prince of Wales* had only just been commissioned, and civilian contractors were still onboard her, trying to fix a problem with one of her turrets. Her crew was also inexperienced, and many of them had joined her just a few weeks before, straight from naval training. Both battleships carried ten 14in. guns, and their armoured belts were meant to be proof against hits from 15in. guns.

The two ships were modern, and benefited from the latest fire-control systems, but while the *King George V* was seen as a reliable weapon of war, the unfinished *Prince of Wales* with her raw crew remained an unknown entity.

The battleship HMS *Rodney*, pictured while turning at high speed. The unusual configuration of her armament was the result of having to limit the size of her armoured belt and her weight in accordance with the inter-war Washington Naval Treaty.

Captain Leach of the *Prince of Wales* had reported that his ship was ready for operational duties, but Tovey knew of the technical problems plaguing the new battleship, and so he was reluctant to allow the *Prince of Wales* to face the *Bismarck* on her own.

The battleship *Rodney* and the older battleship *Ramillies* were escorting Atlantic convoys, and could be diverted if Tovey ordered it. *Rodney* was a Nelson-class battleship, carrying nine 16in. guns in three triple turrets. Her crew was well trained, and had seen action. She could fight the *Bismarck* on equal terms. By contrast *Ramillies* was a modernized World War I battleship, but she carried eight 15in. guns, and, although not fully modernized, her fire-control systems were adequate, and, like all British battleships, she was fitted with radar. If she was backed up by another battleship she could play her part.

Tovey also had battlecruisers at his disposal, the legacy of a flawed notion in naval design where armour was sacrificed for speed. *Repulse* and *Renown* were veterans of World War I, and had been modernized so frequently that sailors nicknamed them *Refit* and *Repair*. They both carried six 15in. guns, which meant they were both under-gunned compared with the *Bismarck*. While *Repulse* served with the Home Fleet, her sister ship *Renown* was part of Force H. Then there was the *Hood*, which was in a class all of her own. She entered service in 1920, but she was never modernized and she retained the light armour associated with a battlecruiser. In particular, her poorly armoured deck, only 3in. thick, made her vulnerable to long-range plunging fire – at ranges of more than 20,000 yards (10 miles) shells plunged almost vertically, meaning they were more likely to hit a deck than a well-armoured belt. Vice Admiral Holland was well aware of this, and it helped shape his tactics – he would order Captain Kerr of the *Hood* and Captain Leach of the *Prince of Wales* to close the range as quickly as possible, until they were safely inside the *Hood*'s 'zone of invulnerability'. This doesn't mean the *Hood* was a liability – far from it. She carried eight well-proven 15in. guns, and she had a well-trained crew. Once the battle began she could be relied upon to play her part in stopping the *Bismarck*.

Just as importantly, the *Hood* was the best-loved warship in the Royal Navy. During the inter-war years the battlecruiser had been used to 'show the flag', touring the world as a floating representative ambassador of the British

Empire. She was perfectly suited to the role, as her sleek lines and elegant profile made her truly beautiful. She was dubbed the 'Mighty *Hood*' by the press, but this ignored the fact that she remained a warship of the 1920s rather than the 1940s.

In theory the aircraft carrier *Victorious* carried 36 aircraft, but that May her hangars were full of crated Hurricane fighters, bound for North Africa. However, she still carried a squadron of Swordfish torpedo bombers, obsolete biplanes crewed by inexperienced, trainee pilots, who had collectively made their first carrier landing just two days before the *Bismarck* left port. Still, these Swordfish represented a powerful offensive weapon, and, despite the lack of training of the aircrews, Tovey knew they might prove vital in the coming battle, as would be the far more experienced aircrews of the *Ark Royal*, which was attached to Force H. *Ark Royal* had the capacity to hold 60 aircraft, and although these were Skua fighters and Swordfish torpedo bombers, she could still launch a decisive air strike when needed.

Finally Royal Air Force and Coastal Command aircraft were available for naval operations as reconnaissance aircraft, or, if need be, as bombers. While these bomber pilots lacked experience of naval operations, they had the capability to launch a devastating air attack if the *Bismarck* were caught at anchor. Tovey therefore had the resources he needed – his real problem was how best to use them, without inviting a disaster if any of his ships or convoys were caught on their own by their powerful German foe.

KRIEGSMARINE

The KMS *Bismarck* was the fourth German warship to bear the name of the 'Iron Chancellor', a symbol of German might and unity. She was the epitome of German engineering prowess, and arguably the most powerful battleship in the world when she first entered service. Design work began on the battleship in 1932, the naval architects drawing on German experiences gained during World War I, but adapted to suit new technology. The German design team had largely ignored the strictures of the Treaty of Versailles, and as a country with no sizeable navy Germany wasn't constrained by the terms of any other international naval treaty. The Versailles treaty had imposed a limit of 35,000 tons, but the designers deliberately breached this ceiling, which meant that the finished battleship exceeded the limit by more than 6,000 tons. Her draught of more than 33ft (10m) barely allowed her to pass through the Kiel Canal – there were just two inches to spare. The canal still dictated the maximum size and displacement of German warships almost half a century after it was opened.

Bismarck was armed with eight 380mm (15in.) guns, produced by Krupp. The original design called for smaller 350mm (13.7in.) guns in accordance with the Treaty of Versailles, but in 1935 the design was modified to accommodate the larger and more powerful weapons. As a result the completed battleship was an extremely well armoured and powerful capital ship.

The *Bismarck* carried her eight 380mm guns in four twin turrets; two forward and two aft, labelled sequentially 'Anton', 'Bruno', 'Caesar' and 'Dora'. They were linked to a superb optical fire-control system, which meant that *Bismarck* could fire her 800kg (1,764lb) projectiles with a higher degree of accuracy than her British counterparts. Their maximum range was 38,000 yards (19 miles). Her secondary armament of 12 150mm (5.9in.) guns were designed for low-angle use against surface targets, but they could also operate against

KMS *Bismarck*, pictured during her working-up exercises in the Baltic in early 1940. The distinctive 'Baltic' camouflage scheme shown here was replaced by an overall mid-grey scheme for Operation *Rheinübung*, deemed more appropriate for the Atlantic Ocean.

aircraft. They shared the same fire-control system as the main armament. Finally she had a suite of 105mm and 20mm anti-aircraft guns, which gave her excellent all-round defence against attacking aircraft.

Her designers had been able to draw on extensive post-war research into the production of face-hardened steel, and the *Bismarck* was protected by a 13in. (325mm) armoured belt of Krupp cementite steel that covered 70 per cent of the ship's hull along the waterline. It also sloped outwards slightly, to increase the effectiveness of the belt. Her upper deck was less well armoured, the result of displacement restrictions. Also, with the exception of her turrets and gun directors, her superstructure was only lightly armoured, which left equipment such as radars, optical gunnery systems and her upper deck passageways vulnerable to enemy fire.

The armoured belt extended well below the waterline to protect the hull of the *Bismarck* from torpedoes, while the hull itself was divided into 22 watertight compartments, all of which could be sealed to prevent flooding from spreading through the ship. She simply sealed off the damaged area, and carried on fighting.

Bismarck was launched by the 'Iron Chancellor' Bismarck's granddaughter in February 1939, an event attended by Hitler and his leading followers. She was a delight to the eye – a warship that combined grace and menace in equal proportions. She was also the pride of the Kriegsmarine. After her sea trials Kapitän Lindemann trained his crew well. By the time Operation *Rheinübung* began her crew were at the peak of efficiency, and ready for anything the Royal Navy and the Atlantic could throw at them.

Her consort was the heavy cruiser KMS *Prinz Eugen*, named after Eugene of Savoy, the 18th-century Imperialist commander who fought alongside the Duke of Marlborough at the battle of Blenheim (1704). She was a cruiser of the Admiral Hipper class, a group of four warships which – like the *Bismarck* – were built in violation of the terms of the Treaty of Versailles. These cruisers were designed to operate deep in the Atlantic as long-range raiders, or as consorts to German capital ships.

She displaced over 14,000 tons, and her appearance was similar to the *Bismarck*, making her effectively a scaled-down version of the larger ship. Her main armament of eight 205mm (8in.) guns was mounted in four twin turrets, and supported by an efficient and modern optical fire control system. She also

The elegant lines of KMS *Prinz Eugen*, armed with eight 8in. guns, mounted in four twin turrets. From a distance she looked similar to KMS *Bismarck*, which caused problems for British gunnery directors during the battle of the Denmark Strait.

carried a secondary armament of eight 105mm (4.1in.) guns, which could be used against both surface and air targets. The *Prinz Eugen* was the third vessel of her class, and she differed slightly from her predecessors, thanks to an improved propulsion system. She was launched in Kiel on August 1938, and was commissioned two years later.

Just before her commissioning she was hit by bombs during an air raid. The damage was minor, and she entered service six weeks later. She was then joined by the *Bismarck* at Gotenhafen, and the two warships trained together. She almost missed Operation *Rheinübung*, as on 24 April she detonated a magnetic mine dropped by a British aircraft just outside Gotenhafen harbour. Again the damage was minor, and she was repaired in two weeks. While the *Bismarck* was powerful enough to take on any British battleship, the *Prinz Eugen* was superior to all British heavy cruisers. With a top speed of 32 knots she could outrun most enemy warships. Taken together, the two German warships were the most modern vessels of their type, and much was expected of them.

Shortly before the Seekampfgruppe sailed several support vessels slipped out of German ports and moved towards their assigned positions in the Arctic Sea and the Atlantic Ocean. The tankers *Heide* and *Weissenburg* were sent into the Arctic in case Lütjens needed to replenish his fuel. Another tanker – the *Wollin* – was stationed at Bergen, ready to replenish the two warships when they reached Norwegian waters. While the Germans could refuel ships at sea, these operations were conducted far more speedily in sheltered coastal waters, and at anchor rather than under way. Additionally, two more fleet tankers (*Belchen* and *Lothringen*) were deployed in the North Atlantic, and two more (*Esso Hamburg* and *Friedrich Breme*) were deployed in mid-Atlantic on the same latitude as the Azores. As well as fuel, these tankers carried extra provisions, ammunition and water, which could extend the range and endurance of the *Bismarck*, giving her the ability to remain at sea for up to eight weeks. Operation *Rheinübung* was an extremely well planned operation.

Finally, Admiral Dönitz, the commander of the Kriegsmarine's U-boat fleet ordered his boats to act as an extra scouting force for Lütjens. Similarly, the Luftwaffe was ready to provide long-range air cover for the battleship in the Western Approaches or in the Norwegian Sea. When the *Bismarck* sailed, Lütjens' staff duly included a U-boat liaison officer and a Luftwaffe staff officer. With his forces in place and his crews ready, all Admiral Lütjens and his men needed was luck.

Ship details of the major participants

KMS *Bismarck*

Commissioned: August 1940

Displacement: 41,673 tons (standard)

Dimensions: length: 823ft, beam: 118ft, draught: 33ft

Maximum speed: 30 knots

Armament: eight 15in. (380mm) guns (4 x 2), 12 5.9in. (150mm) guns (6 x 2), 16 4.1in. (105mm) guns (8 x 2), 16 37mm anti-aircraft guns (8 x 2)

Armour: belt: 12½in., deck 3½in., turrets: 14in. (front), 13in. (rear), 9in. (sides) 7in. (roof), conning tower: 14in.

Complement: 2,065

KMS *Prinz Eugen*

Commissioned: August 1940

Displacement: 16,974 tons (standard)

Dimensions: length: 681ft, beam: 72ft, draught: 20ft

Maximum speed: 32½ knots

Armament: eight 8in. (205mm) guns (4 x 2), 12 4.1in. (105mm) guns (6 x 2), 12 37mm anti-aircraft guns (6 x 2), eight 20mm anti-aircraft guns (8 x 1), 12 21in. (520 mm) torpedo tubes (4 x 3)

Armour: belt: 3¼in., deck: 1¼in., turrets: 6¼in. (front), 4½in. (rear and sides), Conning tower: 6in.

Complement: 1,600

HMS *King George V* and HMS *Prince of Wales*

Commissioned: September 1940 (*King George V*), March 1941 (*Prince of Wales*):

Displacement: 38,031 tons (standard)

Dimensions: length: 745ft, beam: 103ft, draught: 29ft

Maximum speed: 28 knots

Armament: ten 14in. guns (2 x 4, 2 x 2), 16 5¼in. guns (8 x 2), 32 2-pdr pom-poms (4 x 8)

Armour: belt: 15in., deck: 2–6in., turrets: 12¾in. (front), 6¾–8¾in. (sides and rear), conning tower: 4in.

Complement: 1,543

HMS *Hood*

Commissioned: May 1920

Displacement: 42,462 tons (standard)

Dimensions: length: 860½ft, beam: 104ft, draught 28¾ft

Maximum speed: 29½ knots

Armament: eight 15in. guns (4 x 2), eight 4in. guns (4 x 2), 24 2-pdr pom-poms (3x8)

Armour: belt: 5–12in., deck: 1–2in., turrets: 15in. (front), 11–12in. (sides and rear), conning tower: 11in.

Complement: 1,397

HMS *Rodney*

Commissioned: August 1927

Displacement: 42,462 tons (standard), 48,360 tons (fully laden)

Dimensions: length: 860½ft, beam: 104ft, draught 28¾ft

Maximum speed: 23 knots

Armament: nine 16in. guns (3 x 3), 12 6in. guns (6 x 2), six 4.7in. guns (6 x 1), 24 2-pdr pom-poms (3 x 8)

Armour: belt: 14in., deck: 3¾in., turrets: 16in. (front and sides), 9in. (roof), conning tower: 16in. (front and sides)

Complement: 1,397

HMS *Norfolk*, HMS *Dorsetshire*

Commissioned: April 1930 (*Norfolk*), September 1930 (*Dorsetshire*)

Displacement: 10,400 tons (standard)

Dimensions: length: 632ft, beam: 66ft, draught: 17ft

Maximum speed: 32 knots

Armament: eight 8in. guns (4 x 2), eight 4in. guns (4 x 2), 16 2-pdr pom-poms (2 x 8)

Armour: belt: 4½in. deck: 1½in. turrets: 2in., conning tower: 16in. (front and sides)

Complement: 679

HMS *Suffolk*

Commissioned: May 1928

Displacement: 10,310 tons (standard)

Dimensions: length: 630ft, beam: 68ft, draught: 16ft

Maximum speed: 31½ knots

Armament: eight 8in. guns (4 x 2), eight 4in. guns (4 x 2), eight 2-pdr pom-poms (2 x 4)

Armour: belt: 4½in., deck: 1½in., turrets: 2in.

Complement: 679

OPPOSING PLANS

ROYAL NAVY

Vice Admiral Tovey knew that the Germans were planning a major operation, and he knew it would involve a sortie by Bismarck. Increased German radio activity suggested that a sortie was imminent, On the morning of 21 May Tovey had confirmation that the *Bismarck* and the *Prinz Eugen* were on their way, having been sighted in the Kattegat the previous evening. Hours later the German ships were spotted at anchor near Bergen. Tovey laid his plans accordingly.

Essentially, to reach the North Atlantic, the German Seekampfgruppe had to pass through one of three routes. The first was the Denmark Strait, between Greenland and Iceland, while the second lay between Iceland and the Faeroes. Either of these two routes was considered likely, and therefore needed blocking. The final route was between the Faeroes and the Shetland Islands, but this route was considered less likely as the passage lay close to the main British naval base at Scapa Flow.

Another option available to the Germans was to linger in the Arctic Circle, having rendezvoused with one of their tankers. They could then simply wait for Tovey's major warships to return to port to refuel, and then make their move.

Tovey needed to block all these routes, especially the Greenland–Iceland–Faeroes gaps. Rear Admiral Wake-Walker's cruisers *Norfolk* and *Suffolk* were already patrolling the Denmark Strait, while the light cruisers *Arethusa*, *Manchester* and *Birmingham* were in place patrolling the Iceland–Faeroes gap. Just after midnight Tovey ordered Vice Admiral Holland's 'Battlecruiser

LEFT
Rear Admiral Wake-Walker, pictured on board his flagship HMS *Norfolk*. A torpedo specialist, he was regarded as the most able cruiser commander in the Royal Navy. However, he was criticized for not showing more aggression in his shadowing of the *Bismarck*.

RIGHT
A British lookout on board HMS *Suffolk*, photographed at his station while she and *Norfolk* were patrolling the Denmark Strait. While both cruisers were fitted with radar, the sets were temperamental, and so sharp-eyed lookouts remained indispensable during the campaign.

Force' to sea – *Hood* and *Prince of Wales*, escorted by six destroyers. Holland was expected to lie to the south of Iceland, where he could intercept the Germans if they were sighted trying to pass through either of the two gaps. The *King George V*, accompanied by *Renown*, *Victorious*, four cruisers and seven destroyers formed a second line of defence, lying to the south, ready to steam towards the enemy when they were sighted. Apart from that, and the stepping up of reconnaissance flights, all Vice Admiral Tovey could do was wait for the enemy to show their hand.

KRIEGSMARINE

Admiral Lütjens had very clear-cut orders and a well-defined mission. He was ordered to break out into the Atlantic Ocean, and then to attack enemy convoys. The timing, duration and scope of the operation were left to his discretion. He was to avoid taking risks with his ships, which meant where possible he was to avoid fighting enemy capital ships. However, the orders also allowed taking risks if they offered a suitable prize – the destruction of an enemy convoy. The written orders sent to him by Generaladmiral Otto Schniewind and approved by Großadmiral Raeder were extremely detailed, and well worth repeating:

> As soon as the two battleships of the 'Bismarck' Class are ready for deployment we will be able to seek engagement with forces escorting enemy convoys and, when they have been eliminated, destroy the convoy itself. Just now we cannot follow that course, but it would soon be possible, as an intermediate step, for us to use the battleship *Bismarck* to distract the hostile escorting forces, in order to enable the other units engaged to operate against the convoy itself. In the beginning, we will have the advantage of surprise because some other ships involved will be making their first appearance, and, based on his experience on the previous battleship operations, they enemy will assume that one battleship will be enough to defend a convoy.

Wake-Walker's two cruisers were operating on the very edge of the Arctic pack ice. Although taken after the *Bismarck* operation, this rare view of the forecastle of HMS *Suffolk* reflects the even harsher Arctic conditions encountered during the Arctic convoys. (Sullivan Family)

At the earliest possible date, which it is hoped will be during the new moon period of April, the *Bismarck* and the *Prinz Eugen*, led by the Fleet Commander, ought to be deployed as commerce raiders in the Atlantic. At a time that will depend on the completion of the repairs she is currently undergoing, *Gneisenau* will also be sent into the Atlantic.

The lessons learned in the last battleship operation indicate that the *Gneisenau* should join up with the *Bismarck* group, but a diversionary sweep by the *Gneisenau* in the area between Cape Verde and the Azores may be planned before that happens. The heavy cruiser *Prinz Eugen* is to spend most of her time operating tactically with the *Bismarck* or with the *Bismarck* and *Gneisenau*. In contrast to previous directives to the *Gneisenau–Scharnhorst* task force, it is the mission of this task force to also attack escorted convoys. However, the objective of the battleship *Bismarck* should not be to defeat in an all-out engagement enemies of equal strength, but to tie them down in a delaying action, preserving her own combat capability as much as possible, so allowing other ships to attack the merchant vessels in the convoy. The primary mission of this operation also is the destruction of the enemy's merchant shipping; enemy warships will be engaged only when the situation makes it necessary and if can be done without excessive risk.

The operational area will be defined as the entire North Atlantic north of the Equator, with the exception of the territorial waters of neutral states. The Group Commands [i.e Commanders of Baltic or Norwegian theatres] have operational control in their zones. The Fleet Commander [i.e. Lütjens] has control at sea.

During last winter the conduct of the war was fundamentally in accord with the directives of the Seekriegsleitung... and closed with the first extended battleship operation in the open Atlantic. Besides achieving important tactical

The battleship *Bismarck*, lying at anchor just off the quayside at Gotenhafen, shortly before the start of Operation *Rheinübung*. At this angle her sleek, graceful lines are clearly visible – a beautiful but deadly warship, the pride of the Kriegsmarine.

results, this battleship operation shows what important strategic effects similar sorties could have. They would reach beyond the immediate area of operations of the theatres of war. The goal of the war at sea must be to maintain and increase these effects, by repeating such operations as often as possible.

We must not lose sight of the fact that the decisive objective in a struggle with England is to destroy her trade. This can be most effectively accomplished in the North Atlantic, where all her supply lines converge, and where, even in the case of disruption in more distant areas, supplies can still get through via the direct sea route from North America.

Gaining command of the sea in the North Atlantic is the best solution to this problem, but this is not possible with the forces that at this moment we can commit to this purpose, and given the constraint that we must preserve our numerically inferior forces. Nevertheless, we must strive for local and temporary command of the sea in this area and gradually, methodically, and systematically extend it.

During the first battleship operation in the Atlantic, they enemy was always able to deploy one battleship against us, and protect both of its main supply routes. However, it became clear that providing this defence of his convoys brought him to the limit of the possibilities open to him, and the only way he could significantly strengthen his escort forces is by weakening areas important to him or by reducing convoy sailings.

These orders reveal a lot about the way Raeder and Schniewind were gradually modifying the way the major surface units were used. In 1939 the *Graf Spee* was largely left to her own devices, and used in a similar manner to the way German light cruisers had been used as surface raiders in 1914. Subsequent sorties had become increasingly complex, as the German capital ships had to break through the British cordon which ran from Greenland to Orkney, and then sustain themselves for a limited spell in the midst of Britain's transatlantic shipping lanes, before returning to a friendly port.

In the Operation *Rheinübung* orders, the emphasis was still on commerce raiding, but for once the German task force would be powerful enough to engage protected convoys directly, especially if the escorts were merely destroyers or cruisers. This is what was meant by 'without excessive risk'. However, German naval intelligence was well aware that several convoys were being escorted by British battleships, and Raeder was unwilling that Lütjens be drawn into a stand-up duel with these powerful ships. He left the operational decision of where and when to attack to Lütjens, but it was clear that the main object of the operation was to sink enemy merchant ships, and so help bring Britain to her knees through the strangling of her mercantile lifelines. Risking major German surface units in surface actions against enemy battleships was both unnecessary and risky.

Finally, the intriguing passage about control of the seas is misleading. Raeder and Schniewind weren't contemplating the destruction of the British Home Fleet. That would have been nigh-on impossible. Instead, they were advocating the establishment of temporary control of the transatlantic sea lanes by forcing the British to keep their convoys in port until the German task force withdrew. This establishment of temporary naval dominance could then be repeated during future operations, until the whole convoy system was brought to a halt.

Admiral Lütjens read all this, and made his own plans. He was also well aware that once he left Norwegian waters, he and his men were on their own.

THE CAMPAIGN

THE BREAK-OUT

On the quayside the onlookers watched as the *Bismarck* slipped her cables and edged out into Gotenhafen (Gdynia) harbour. As the tugs pulled her head round, the ship's band on her quarterdeck struck up *Muß i' denn* ('Wooden Heart'), a song traditionally played at the start of a long voyage. The great battleship didn't steam very far – within half an hour she was riding at anchor in the mouth of the harbour, where a procession of barges laden with provisions, ammunition, fuel and water took turns to come alongside her and unload their supplies. At 2am on Monday 19 May the *Bismarck* and her consort *Prinz Eugen* finally raised their anchors, and they headed out to sea. Operation *Rheinübung* was finally under way.

Once in the Baltic Sea the two ships headed west, leaving the low Polish coast behind them as they set a course for Cape Arkona on the German island of Rügen. At noon they rendezvoused with two destroyers that were waiting off the island. The ships continued westwards, rounding the Danish island of Lolland to enter the Femer Belt between Denmark and Germany, and rendezvousing with a third destroyer, the flotilla leader. By midnight they were threading their way northwards through Danish waters, and by 2am the ships entered the Great Belt, the passage between Funen and Zealand that

The Swedish seaplane-carrying cruiser *Gotland* sighted the *Bismarck* during the afternoon of 20 May, as the German force was steaming through the Kattegat, heading for the Norwegian coast. The *Gotland* reported the sighting to the Swedish naval headquarters in Stockholm.

led to the Kattegat, and the North Sea beyond. The transit of this narrow channel was uneventful, and as dawn rose on the morning of 20 May the *Bismarck* and her consorts entered the Kattegat, with the German-occupied Danish peninsula on one side, and the coast of neutral Sweden on the other. Low cloud cover reduced the risk of being spotted by British reconnaissance aircraft. However, Lütjens was well aware that the British had other ways to gather information.

Sweden might have been neutral, but her sympathies lay with the Allies. Therefore, while Admiral Lütjens was worried that any of the Danish or Swedish fishing boats he steamed past might have reported seeing the Seekampfgruppe, when at noon he encountered the Swedish cruiser *Gotland* he was certain that the sighting report would be radioed to Stockholm, and passed on to the British. Sure enough, that evening the British Embassy in Stockholm passed on the sighting report to the Admiralty. Meanwhile Lütjens had passed through the Kattegat into the Skagerrak, and the rougher waters of the North Sea. Minesweepers led them safely through the mined waters during the late afternoon.

Captain Henry Denham RN, the British Naval Attaché in Stockholm, who, despite harassment by German agents, managed to send word to the Admiralty that the *Bismarck* and *Prinz Eugen* had passed through the Kattegat together, heading towards the Norwegian Sea.

The ships then headed west again, aiming for the southern tip of Norway near Kristiansand, which they rounded during the night. Dawn on 21 May found them off Stavanger on the Norwegian coast, heading north. At noon the Seekampfgruppe entered the Korsfjord, and steamed up the inlet towards the port of Bergen. That morning the *Prinz Eugen* intercepted a British radio signal telling aircraft to search for two battleships and three destroyers on a northerly course off the coast of Southern Norway. Lütjens now knew he had been spotted.

Indeed he had. The news had reached the Admiralty, who immediately passed it on to Vice Admiral Tovey in Scapa Flow. At 11am, as the *Bismarck* anchored in the Grimstadfjord, a small inlet of the Korsfjord to the south of Bergen, Tovey was digesting the news in his cabin on board the *King George V*. News of the *Bismarck* had actually come from three sources. First an agent in Gotenhafen had sent a message to London, reporting that the *Bismarck* had sailed. Then came the message from the British Naval Attaché in Stockholm that the *Gotland* had spotted the *Bismarck* and another large ship in the Kattegat. Finally came word from the Norwegian resistance, which said the two ships and their destroyer escort had been sailing past Kristiansand. Reconnaissance planes were now scouring the Norwegian fjords between Stavanger and Bergen.

At 1.15pm Flying Officer Suckling of Coastal Command flew up the Korsfjord at 8,000ft (2,440m), and turned into the Grimstadfjord. He wasn't spotted, as the German ships never opened fire, and his Spitfire flew on unmolested, taking pictures of the scene below. The *Bismarck* lay at anchor, while a few miles to the north the *Prinz Eugen* was taking on fuel in Kalvanes Bay. That afternoon Kapitän Brinkmann of the *Prinz Eugen* refuelled his ship from the tanker *Wollin*, but Kapitän Lindemann felt he had sufficient fuel on board, and declined the offer to replenish his oil tanks. These operations were inherently risky, particularly if the battleship came under air attack during the replenishment. However, the decision not to refuel the *Bismarck* would have serious implications on the course of the campaign. The crews of both ships also spent the afternoon painting over their distinctive 'Baltic camouflage' schemes, whose main feature were chevron-shaped stripes amidships. These would have made the ships easier to spot against the grey of the North Atlantic, and so they were replaced with a standard hull grey.

Operation *Rheinübung*

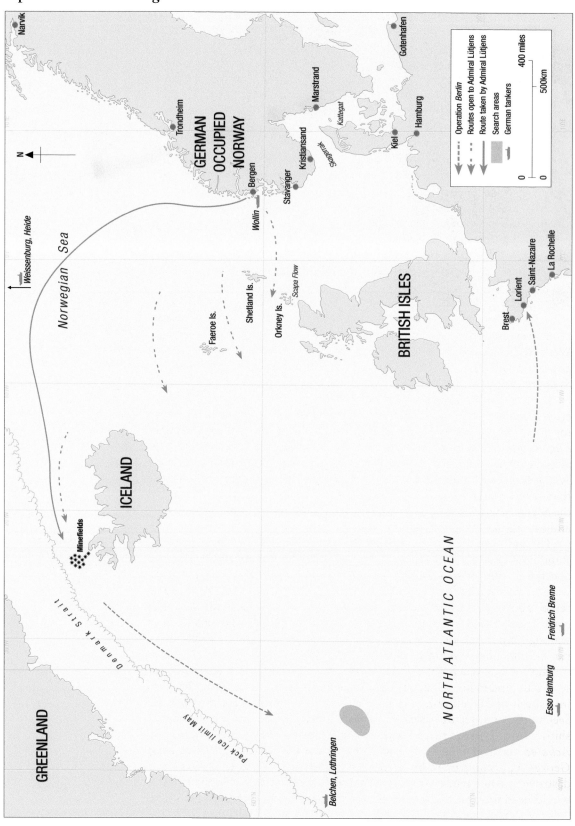

British cruisers were already patrolling the Denmark Strait. Rear Admiral Wake-Walker, commanding the 1st Cruiser Squadron, had the two heavy cruisers *Norfolk*, his flagship, and her near sister *Suffolk*. On 19 May the *Suffolk* had put into the Hvalfjord in Iceland to refuel, and Tovey ordered her to hurry back to rejoin the *Norfolk*. Both ships were County-class heavy cruisers, armed with eight 8in. guns apiece. With a displacement of 10,000 tons and a top speed of 31 knots, they were comparable in size to the *Prinz Eugen*, but they were two decades older and less well armoured, and they also lacked the German cruiser's modern gunnery directors. Still, Wake-Walker's job was to locate the German ships and then shadow them, rather than try to engage them in battle. They also carried radar, which gave them the edge in this kind of warfare. In effect, the two cruisers were Tovey's eyes and ears in the waters to the west of Iceland.

The light cruiser *Arethusa* was also at Hvalfjord, and she was put on standby to sail east or west, as circumstances demanded. Between Iceland and the Faeroes two more light cruisers – *Birmingham* and *Manchester* – were on patrol, and Tovey ordered them to put into Iceland's Skaalfjord to refuel, allowing them to return to their patrol positions before the *Bismarck* could reach them. That way he reduced the risk of the *Bismarck* simply waiting until the British cruisers ran out of fuel before he tried to make his run into the North Atlantic.

Next, Tovey ordered Vice Admiral Holland in the *Hood* to take the *Prince of Wales* under his wing, and sail towards the south coast of Iceland, just south of Havelfjord, where he could move to intercept the German Seekampfgruppe regardless of which side of Iceland it sailed. The two capital ships would be escorted by six destroyers: *Electra*, *Echo*, *Anthony*, *Icarus*, *Achates* and *Antelope*. Tovey planned to sail the following day in *King George V*, accompanied by *Victorious* and a small force of cruisers and destroyers. After rendezvousing with the *Repulse* off the Western Isles, he would head towards the west-north-west, to cover the convoys at sea in the Atlantic, and to provide distant cover for Vice Admiral Holland.

LEFT
The crucial photograph of the *Bismarck* in Grimstadfjord, taken on 21 May by a Spitfire Reconnaissance plane of Coastal Command piloted by Flying Officer Michael Suckling. The photo also shows the battleship, accompanied by three supply tenders. (Imperial War Museum, London)

RIGHT
While *Bismarck* anchored in the Grimstadfjord, the *Prinz Eugen* – the largest ship in this British aerial reconnaissance photograph – anchored off Kalvenes in the Hjelte Fjord, a few miles to the north. She is surrounded by tenders and refuelling vessels.

Admiral Lütjens was also planning his next move. An aerial reconnaissance of Scapa Flow told him that most of Tovey's capital ships were still in port, so it looked as if his presence in Norwegian waters might have gone undetected. He therefore still had the advantage of surprise on his side. If he were to break out into the North Atlantic he would need to pass through one of four passages. The most northerly route was the Denmark Strait, between Iceland and Greenland. This had the advantage of being the furthest away from Scapa Flow, but the Strait itself was narrower than shown on the charts because pack ice off the Greenland coast and the possibility of mines off the Icelandic coast meant he had to keep pretty much in the middle of the passage.

The second route lay between Iceland and the Faeroe Islands, and, although British cruisers would probably guard the route, it was the most direct of the passages and the one recommended by Generaladmiral Schniewind. A third passage between the Faeroes and Shetland was also a possibility, although its proximity to Scapa Flow made this one a really hazardous undertaking. The fourth gap, between Shetland and Orkney was so close to Scapa Flow and the airbases on Orkney that it was virtually suicidal. Effectively, Lütjens' only two options were the Denmark Strait and the Iceland–Faeroes gap.

Lütjens was well aware that Raeder and Schniewind favoured the route between Iceland and the Faeroes. He now thought that this route was too risky. He was worried that his presence in Norwegian waters might have been reported, and that the British had already left Scapa Flow and were steaming north to intercept him. The final decision lay with him, as his orders had given him full operational control. After due consideration Lütjens opted for the more distant of the two routes. He was confident he could deal with any cruiser screen in the Denmark Strait, and there was a good chance that his task force could pass through the gap before the British could send capital ships there to bar his way into the North Atlantic. He didn't realize that just hours after the reconnaissance flight, Vice Admiral Holland was preparing to lead his force out into the Atlantic.

On the evening of 21 May, the *Bismarck* weighed anchor and steamed north up the Hjeltefjord, the northern continuation of the Korsfjord. She was joined by the *Prinz Eugen* and the two destroyers, and then followed the fjord towards the open sea. Once in the rougher waters of the Norwegian Sea she turned towards the north. At midnight she was still heading northwards at 24 knots, towards the Arctic Ocean. At 4.20am the accompanying destroyers were detached, and they put in to the German naval base at Trondheim to refuel. The two larger ships were now left on their own. Apart from Lütjens and his immediate staff, nobody really knew which route the Seekampfgruppe would take, or when the men would experience their first taste of battle.

Shortly after 1pm on 22 May the *Bismarck* and *Prinz Eugen* altered course towards the west, bound for the north of Iceland. They were now north of the Arctic Circle. That meant they were heading for the Denmark Strait. Although the German tanker *Weissenburg* was stationed in their path, Lütjens made no attempt to rendezvous with her. He therefore missed *Bismarck*'s last chance to take on more fuel. With hindsight this was a mistake, but Lütjens was clearly a man in a hurry. He wanted to reach the passage on the far side of Iceland before the British Home Fleet arrived.

Officially, Iceland was a Danish possession, albeit one with a large degree of independence. When the Germans invaded Denmark the previous spring the British occupied the island, turning it into a bastion of free Denmark. The island also became a superbly placed base for the British, sitting astride Germany's

two most viable routes into the Atlantic Ocean. Since September 1939 the Royal Navy had turned several of Iceland's harbours into refuelling and supply bases. The largest of these was in the Hvalfjord, beside Reykjavik, but other smaller naval bases were also available at Akureyri on the north coast, and Seydisfjord on the eastern side of the island. A brigade of British infantry was also stationed in Iceland, to defend the island against any threat of invasion.

The pack ice off the coast of Greenland reduced the width of the navigable channel in the Denmark Strait to between 60 and 100 miles, depending on the time of year. In May 1941 it was around 90 miles (167km) wide. To limit the German options even further the Royal Navy laid minefields at the northern end of the Denmark Strait, close to the Icelandic coast. The Germans knew that the British had left a narrow channel close to the pack ice, and it was into this narrow waterway that the two German ships were heading. It was no more than 30 miles (56km) wide.

It was also where Wake-Walker's cruisers were patrolling – the *Norfolk* on station at the edge of the minefield, and the *Suffolk* steaming north to join her, after refuelling in Hvalfjord. Late on 21 May the Admiralty signalled

Wake-Walker with the news that the *Bismarck* and an Admiral Hipper-class heavy cruiser were likely to attempt a passage through Icelandic waters during the next few days. With the prospect of a powerful German battleship appearing through the icy mist, the British lookouts and radar operators kept their eyes peeled for the first sign of the enemy.

The British still didn't know the identity of the Admiral Hipper-class heavy cruiser that accompanied the *Bismarck*, but they knew she was powerful enough to augment the firepower of the *Bismarck* in a naval battle fought at a range of less than 10 miles (19km). That gave the German battleship a decided advantage in a duel against another battleship. Tovey knew this, which is why he decided to send his capital ships in pairs – *Hood* and *Prince of Wales*, and his own flagship *King George V* and the battlecruiser *Repulse*, which was steaming north from the Clyde to join him.

Jut before midnight on 21 May, at roughly the same time as the *Bismarck* was sailing north up the Norwegian coast, Vice Admiral Holland's 'Battlecruiser Force' raised anchor in Scapa Flow and began their voyage out through Hoxa Sound into the Pentland Firth, then the Atlantic. With Holland's force placed to cover either the Denmark Strait or the Iceland–Faeroes Gap, Tovey was making the best possible use of the ships he had at his disposal. Whichever way the *Bismarck* went, Holland would be there to intercept her.

The British heavy cruisers *Norfolk* and *Suffolk* in the Denmark Strait, and the light cruisers *Arethusa*, *Birmingham* and *Manchester* to the east of Iceland were all too poorly armed to take on the *Bismarck*. The light cruisers, with their 6in. guns were particularly vulnerable, as they also lacked the firepower to damage the *Prinz Eugen*. Fortunately the job of both cruiser forces wasn't to go down fighting, but to locate the enemy, and then use their radars to shadow the German Seekampfgruppe from a safe distance. They would then radio any changes in the enemy's course and speed, allowing Holland to race forwards to intercept the Bismarck before she reached the Atlantic. As a safeguard, Tovey's ships would move forward too, just in case the Germans managed to evade Holland's force.

That evening RAF bombers flew up the Korsfjord to bomb the *Bismarck* as she lay at anchor, but poor visibility meant that they never saw their target. They dropped their bombs over the Grimstadfjord anyway, hoping to hit their target by luck rather than accuracy. By that time the fjord was empty, as was Kalvanes Bay where the *Prinz Eugen* had anchored to take on fuel. The German Seekampfgruppe had already sailed. When the bombers appeared the *Bismarck* was already in the Norwegian Sea, heading north towards the Arctic Circle. Late the following afternoon a reconnaissance aircraft managed to fly under the cloud to discover that both anchorages were empty. It had now been almost 30 hours since the *Bismarck* and the *Prinz Eugen* had last been seen. The German ships could have travelled over 600 miles (1,110km) in that time, which meant they could already be approaching Iceland.

While the low cloud and bad weather had hindered the RAF, it also worked in Tovey's favour. Another German reconnaissance flight on 22 May reported that the capital ships of the Home Fleet were still at anchor in Scapa Flow. A combination of cloud and dummy warships made of wood and canvas had fooled the German aircrew. That means that both sides didn't know where the enemy was. As darkness fell on 22 May the only bright spot for Vice Admiral Tovey was that he knew the enemy was at sea, and almost certainly steaming heading towards his screen of cruisers.

TOP
Weather conditions in the Denmark Strait in late May 1941 were far from ideal, with heavy seas and poor visibility. However, conditions improved by the time the *Bismarck* encountered the *Hood*. This view is taken from the bridge of HMS *Suffolk*.

BOTTOM
HMS *Hood*, on her way to intercept the *Bismarck* in the Denmark Strait, photographed the evening before her loss, from the top of *Prince of Wales'* 'A' turret. At the time the two ships were to the south of Iceland.

At 11pm Tovey sailed from Scapa Flow in *King George V*, accompanied by the aircraft carrier *Victorious*, five light cruisers (*Aurora*, *Galatea*, *Hermione*, *Kenya* and *Neptune*) and six destroyers. The *Repulse* was ordered to steam northwards at full speed to join the rest of the force. That meant that during the night of 22–23 May two groups of British capital ships were heading towards Iceland, with Holland's Battlecruiser Force a day's steaming ahead of Tovey. To the north, beyond the Arctic Circle, *Bismarck* and *Prinz Eugen* were steaming westwards, towards the Denmark Strait. Lütjens still thought the Home Fleet was back in Scapa Flow, rather than steaming west at full speed to intercept him.

During the morning of 23 May, as Tovey's force was joined by the *Repulse* to the north of the Western Isles, Lütjens was already approaching the northern end of the Denmark Strait. Late that afternoon lookouts on board the *Bismarck* sighted the edge of the pack ice off Greenland, and, at 6pm, Lütjens ordered his ships to turn towards the south-south-east with the two ships in line astern, with *Bismarck* leading the way. As Lütjens didn't know how far west the British minefield extended he skirted as close as he could to the edge of the pack ice on the western edge of the Strait.

Break-out into the Atlantic

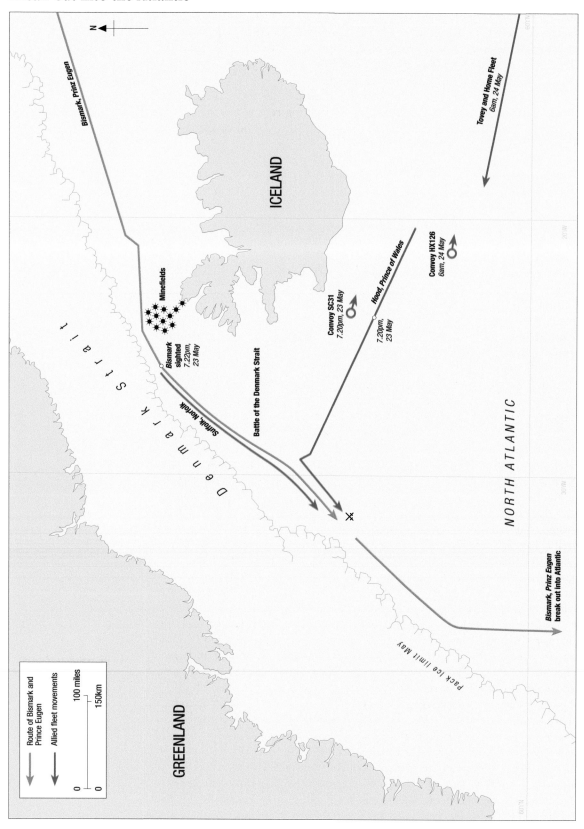

For his part, Tovey could now discount that the Germans were trying to break through into the Atlantic through one of the passages to the south of the Faeroes. The whole area had been crossed and re-crossed by reconnaissance aircraft – if the *Bismarck* was heading that way, she would have been spotted. That left the Iceland–Faeroes gap, and the Denmark Strait. Tovey suspected that the *Bismarck* was heading towards the westernmost passage, but he couldn't gamble on his hunch. He still needed to be prepared for all eventualities. What he really needed was a sighting report from one of his cruisers. Then he would know where the *Bismarck* was, and could send his two main forces to block her path.

THE BATTLE OF THE DENMARK STRAIT

The moment Vice Admiral Tovey had been waiting for came at 7.22pm in the evening of Friday 23 May. Unusually clear conditions meant that visibility in the Denmark Strait that evening was as high as 8 miles (15km), although patches of icy mist made sighting a matter of luck. Lookouts on board the *Suffolk* saw the German battleship looming out of the mist, at a range of 7 miles (13km). The mist closed in again, and Captain Ellis ordered his cruiser to turn away and hide in the mist to the south-east, close to the edge of the minefield. The British cruiser had a troublesome radar set, which explained why the lookouts spotted the enemy first.

The *Bismarck* had radar too, albeit a more primitive kind – an FuMG 40G active radar – with a much shorter range. It still detected *Suffolk* though, and Kapitän Lindemann ordered his crew to action stations. Ellis radioed the news to the Admiralty, who relayed it to Tovey and Holland. An hour later Ellis in *Suffolk* was joined by Rear Admiral Wake-Walker in *Norfolk*, and the two cruisers tried to shadow the enemy force. Lookouts on board the *Bismarck* spotted *Norfolk*, and opened fire at a range of just 6 miles (11km). Captain Phillips of the *Norfolk* scurried for cover, and like the *Suffolk* she hid in the mist, relying on her radar to keep her distance, while still remaining on the *Bismarck*'s tail. By that time Suffolk's Type 284 fire-control radar had been repaired, and although it had a range of only 10 miles (19km), it was still better than the Type 286M search radar set carried by *Norfolk*. *Suffolk* therefore became the electronic hunter, and the *Bismarck* the quarry. This game of cat and mouse continued after darkness fell, and Wake-Walker's cruisers sent a steady stream of reports, which allowed Tovey and Holland to plot courses to intercept the enemy.

During the brief exchange of fire with *Norfolk* the blast from her own 15in. guns damaged the *Bismarck*'s forward-looking FuMG 40G active radar, which meant she was unable to detect targets ahead of her. Lütjens therefore ordered the *Prinz Eugen* to forge ahead and take the lead – a switch of order that would have a major effect in the coming battle. The radar operators in the shadowing British cruisers never noticed the change. The encounter with the two cruisers was what Lütjens had expected – he knew the British would maintain a cruiser screen in the Denmark Strait. However, he also believed that the British had been slow to react to the German sortie, and he expected to pass through the channel into the North Atlantic before any British capital ships could intervene. In fact, *Hood* and *Prince of Wales* were less than 300 miles (555km) away, and closing fast.

On board the *Hood*, when Vice Admiral Holland heard that the *Bismarck* had been sighted he worked out the positions of the two forces on the chart, then ordered an increase of speed to 27 knots, and altered course to 295 degrees. His plan was to intercept the German ships before dawn the following day. He knew that, despite their individual handicaps, the *Hood* and the untried *Prince of Wales* could take on the *Bismarck*, while Wake-Walker's two cruisers could keep the *Prinz Eugen* occupied. At least on paper it looked like he would enjoy a superiority of both numbers and firepower over his German opponent. The rough seas meant that at that speed the accompanying destroyers were unable to keep up. Therefore at 10pm Holland detached them, ordering them to follow as best they could and to wait for further orders.

About the same time, the radar operators on *Suffolk* saw that the German ships had changed course. The *Bismarck* had reversed course in an attempt to attack or drive off the two shadowing cruisers. The radar gave the British ships warning, and they simply slipped away under cover of the fog. Unable to spot them, the *Bismarck* resumed her original course, with *Prinz Eugen* still leading. The British cruisers resumed their position astern of her, but two hours later, just after midnight, a snowstorm temporarily blinded *Suffolk*'s radar. All the operator saw was a blur. By coincidence Admiral Lütjens chose roughly the same moment to increase speed. As a result the Germans slipped ahead under cover of the snowstorm, and the British cruisers lost contact. It was a full three hours before radar contact was regained.

In the meantime Holland altered course to 240 degrees – the south-west – in case the Germans changed course as well as speed. That way he was surer of an interception, only that it would take place a little after dawn. As Holland's force steamed west to intercept his crews went to action stations, where his men grabbed what sleep they could. On the *Prince of Wales*, the few civilian contractors who were still on board worked through the night to sort out the mechanical problems that still plagued the main guns. As dawn approached, the lookouts peered through the darkness to starboard, waiting for the first sign of the enemy warships they knew were out there.

At 5.37am a lookout on board the *Hood* spotted smoke on the horizon, directly on the starboard beam of the battlecruiser. Then a small black speck appeared underneath the smoke. It had to be the *Bismarck*. The main gunnery director computed that the range was 30,000 yards (15 miles), which was beyond the effective gunnery range of both *Hood* and *Prince of Wales*. The crews were already at action stations, and the guns were now trained round onto the new target. It was now a matter of waiting until the range decreased enough to open fire.

On the *Bismarck* and *Prinz Eugen* Admiral Lütjens had also kept his crews at their battle stations throughout the night in case the British cruisers were spotted. He still thought that the Home Fleet was in Scapa Flow, and that his route into the Atlantic was clear. He knew that the British cruisers would have told the Admiralty that the German Seekampfgruppe had been sighted, and he expected Vice Admiral Tovey to be heading his way. However, Lütjens still thought the nearest British capital ships were at least a day's steaming away. It therefore came as a complete surprise when just after 5am the sound of unknown ships to the south were picked up on *Prinz Eugen*'s sonar. Then, at 5.37am, lookouts on the German cruiser spotted smoke on the horizon, on the same bearing as the sonar contact.

Like Vice Admiral Holland, Admiral Lütjens looked down at his plotting table. The detected ships were about 70 degrees off his port bow, almost on his port beam. The enemy were sailing at right angles to him, which meant they would probably land up ahead of the German ships, 'crossing their T' if it came to a gunnery duel. That meant that while they could fire all their guns at the Germans, only the forward-facing guns of the *Prinz Eugen* could fire back. Lütjens still doubted that the contacts were capital ships – more likely they were British cruisers, sent to relieve those who were shadowing him.

If they were battleships then Lütjens hoped the superior speed of his ships would keep him out of danger, allowing him to circle round the enemy to reach the Atlantic. After all, his mission was to destroy enemy convoys, not to risk his force in a pounding sea battle. Only the British battlecruisers like the *Hood*, or the modern battleships of the King George V class had the speed to force a battle. The next few minutes would prove crucial, and would tell Lütjens just what kind of enemy he was facing.

In theory the 15in. guns carried by the *Hood* had a maximum range of 30,000 yards (15 miles), but her gunnery director could engage targets only up 26,500 yards (13 miles). That was extreme range, and the chances of hitting anything were minimal. The standard doctrine was to hold fire until the target was less than 25,000 yards (12 miles) away. Even then the chance of a single hit on target from a full eight-gun salvo was less than one in five.

When the smoke was sighted Captain Kerr of the *Hood* would have ordered his gunnery officer to calculate the range, bearing and angles of fire, which allowed Vice Admiral Holland to decide upon his tactics. He knew he had a superiority of two to one in heavy ordnance, but that the gun crews on the *Prince of Wales* were inexperienced, her guns were faulty and his own flagship was vulnerable to long-range plunging fire. As the range decreased the accuracy of fire would improve, and the *Hood* would become less vulnerable to plunging

The 'mighty *Hood*' looked impressive, but her greatest weakness was her poor deck armour, which was particularly vulnerable to plunging fire at long range. Vice Admiral Holland wanted to close with the *Bismarck* as quickly as possible, to reduce this risk.

The *Bismarck* opening fire on the *Hood*, photographed from the stern of *Prinz Eugen* during the opening stages of the battle of the Denmark Strait. The photograph was taken around 5.55am, when the *Bismarck* was firing her highly accurate opening salvo.

fire. *Hood*'s 'zone of vulnerability' to plunging fire extended for another 8,000 yards (7,300m), meaning it was vital that the battlecruiser closed to within 18,000 yards (9 miles) as quickly as possible. His other consideration was that he wanted to keep between the German ships and the Atlantic.

When the enemy ships were sighted the two British warships were steaming in line astern, with the *Hood* in the lead, and the *Prince of Wales* following her 800 yards (730m) astern. Their course was 240 degrees – west-south-west – and their speed was a racy 28 knots. The Germans were on almost a parallel course, steering 222 degrees – south-west – with the *Prinz Eugen* in the lead, and the *Bismarck* following her 1,000 yards (910m) astern. At that angle and range the German ships could still evade Holland by turning to starboard, but so far they continued on the same course. At 5.37am, soon after the sighting was made, Holland ordered *Hood* to turn to starboard onto a new course of 280 degrees, which would close the range a little faster. *Prince of Wales* followed the flagship. Within five minutes of the turn, the two columns of ships would be in range of each other.

Lütjens noticed that the British ships had turned slightly towards him. That was something of a shock, as no cruisers would deliberately come within gun range so willingly. That meant the two ships approaching him had to be capital ships. Worse news was to follow. The *Bismarck*'s fire-control team had been monitoring the enemy ships for a few minutes now, and it was clear they were approaching at high speed – around 28 knots. The only British capital ships capable of such speeds were the *Hood*, the two Renown-class battlecruisers, or one of the new battleships of the King George V class. He was left with no option but to fight. At 5.39am he turned away slightly onto a new course of 265 degrees – almost due west. That put the two columns of ships on slightly converging courses, about 26,000 yards (13 miles) away from each other. It also slowed the rate of closure, giving Lütjens a little more time to work out exactly who was attacking him.

The battle of the Denmark Strait

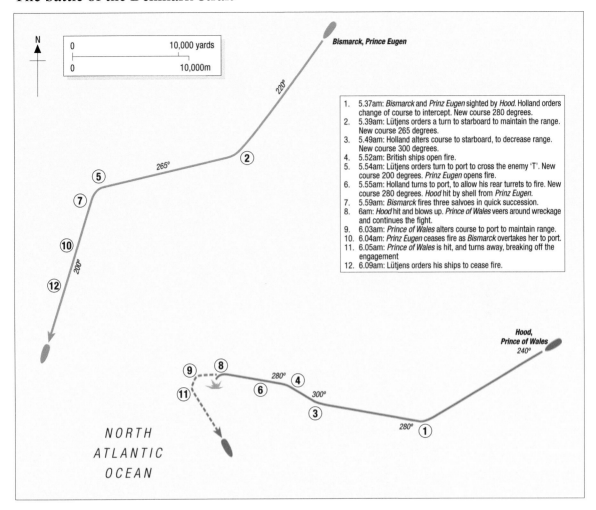

Scale: 0 — 10,000 yards / 0 — 10,000m

N

Bismarck, Prince Eugen

1. 5.37am: *Bismarck* and *Prinz Eugen* sighted by *Hood*. Holland orders change of course to intercept. New course 280 degrees.
2. 5.39am: Lütjens orders a turn to starboard to maintain the range. New course 265 degrees.
3. 5.49am: Holland alters course to starboard, to decrease range. New course 300 degrees.
4. 5.52am: British ships open fire.
5. 5.54am: Lütjens orders turn to port to cross the enemy 'T'. New course 200 degrees. *Prinz Eugen* opens fire.
6. 5.55am: Holland turns to port, to allow his rear turrets to fire. New course 280 degrees. *Hood* hit by shell from *Prinz Eugen*.
7. 5.59am: *Bismarck* fires three salvoes in quick succession.
8. 6am: *Hood* hit and blows up. *Prince of Wales* veers around wreckage and continues the fight.
9. 6.03am: *Prince of Wales* alters course to port to maintain range.
10. 6.04am: *Prinz Eugen* ceases fire as *Bismarck* overtakes her to port.
11. 6.05am: *Prince of Wales* is hit, and turns away, breaking off the engagement
12. 6.09am: Lütjens orders his ships to cease fire.

Hood, Prince of Wales

NORTH ATLANTIC OCEAN

The British gunnery officers reported the course change to Holland. Less than ten minutes after Lütjens changed course Holland did the same, turning to starboard onto a new heading of 300 degrees. The trouble was, this new course meant that the aft guns on both British ships couldn't fire, as the guns couldn't train far enough ahead to engage the enemy. This meant the British ships lost almost half of their firepower, but it reduced the time the *Hood* remained within its 'zone of vulnerability' for plunging fire. The German ships were now 40 degrees to starboard of the British flagship, but the angle was decreasing as the range closed. Once within the *Hood*'s 'zone of invulnerability' when the range dropped to 18,000 yards (9 miles), Holland planned to alter course to port, to put his two ships on a parallel course to his German opponents.

At 5.52am the range had decreased to 25,000 yards (12 miles), and Captain Kerr of the *Hood* gave the order to open fire. The *Prince of Wales* fired her first salvo of six 14in. shells less than a minute later. At that range it took 50 seconds for the salvo to reach its target. Once it landed the gunnery officer would note where the shell splashes fell, then correct his aim. In 1941 gunnery was a process of gradual refinement as the range was corrected with every salvo until falling shells straddled the target. Then only minor corrections were needed to

LEFT
An accurate salvo of 15in. shells from HMS *Hood* falls a short distance astern of the *Prinz Eugen* during the opening exchanges of the battle of the Denmark Strait. A minute later the *Hood* switched targets to engage the *Bismarck*.

RIGHT
The moment HMS *Hood* blew up, viewed from the *Prinz Eugen*, some 10 miles (19km) away. Two distinct columns of smoke can be seen, with the smoke on the far left caused by the guns of the *Prince of Wales*.

make sure that the guns continued to track the enemy ship as it moved. Once straddled it was only a matter of time before shells began hitting the enemy ship, and ripping through its decks at long range, or the armoured belt if the range was shorter. The only problem was that the *Hood* was firing her guns at the wrong target.

Holland ordered both of his ships to concentrate their fire on the leading German ship, which he thought was the *Bismarck*. The trouble was, at that range and angle, the *Bismarck* and the *Prinz Eugen* had a very similar silhouette, and the difference in size between them was negligible at such a great range. In other words, the British gunnery officers were unable to tell which of the enemy ships was the battleship, and which was the heavy cruiser. Convention dictated that the *Bismarck* would be in the lead, where it was better placed to protect the less well-armoured vessel. As the two German ships had swapped places during the night owing to the *Bismarck*'s faulty radar, the British were firing on the *Prinz Eugen*, not the *Bismarck*.

Actually, just before the *Hood* opened fire, the gunnery officer on the *Prince of Wales* noticed the mistake. The optics used in the fire-control director of the modern battleship were much better than those in the *Hood*, and he was able to see that the second enemy ship was larger than the leading one. He reported his discovery to Captain Leach, who therefore faced something of a dilemma. He trusted his gunnery officer, but his orders were to engage the leading enemy ship. It would take at least a minute to make the calculations necessary to engage the new target, so the stakes were high. Leach decided to follow his instincts rather than his orders, and he ordered his gunnery officers to switch targets onto the second ship – the *Bismarck*. Unfortunately, the discovery was never radioed to the *Hood*, which continued to fire at the *Prinz Eugen*.

At 5.53am shell splashes were spotted in front of the leading German ship – the *Hood*'s first salvo had fallen slightly short. A minute later the same thing happened to the *Bismarck*, as the *Prince of Wales*' first salvo landed short. On both British ships the gunnery officers recalculated everything, and ordered the guns to shoot again. The splash made by a 15in. shell was markedly different to that made by a 6in. or an 8in. one. Any lingering doubts that the British ships weren't capital ships vanished when Lütjens saw the huge shell splashes.

He immediately gave the order to change course to port, to confuse the British gunnery directors. The new course was 200 degrees, which meant that the two sides were converging even faster than before – at a rate of almost 1,000 yards a minute. When he ordered the turn the German ships were almost directly ahead of the British column, which was 23,000 yards (11 miles) away to the south-east. The course change ensured that the Germans would 'cross the T' of the British ships. The Germans could still fire all their guns at the British, while the British could not, which temporarily cancelled out Holland's superiority in numbers. Four British guns were now firing on each German ship – the firepower of the *Prince of Wales* having been reduced after her first salvo when one of her guns in 'B' turret malfunctioned, and remained out of action for the rest of the battle.

By contrast, the *Bismarck* could fire all eight guns at the leading British ship – the *Hood* – while the *Prinz Eugen* was now just inside the maximum range for her own lighter 8in. guns. While she mightn't be able to penetrate the *Hood*'s belt armour when the range decreased, at 23,000 yards (11 miles) she had an outside chance of landing a plunging hit on the deck of the enemy battlecruiser. Lütjens also ordered both ships to open fire as soon as the turn was completed.

In fact the *Prinz Eugen* opened fire before the *Bismarck*, at 5.54am, as she was the first of the two ships to complete her turn to port. By then the range was down to 23,000 yards. Amazingly, she scored a hit with her first salvo – a testimony to the effectiveness of German optical rangefinders. One of her eight 8in. shells hit an ammunition locker on the upper deck of the *Hood*, used to store shells for her 4in. guns. This first hit caused no real damage, but it showed that the *Prinz Eugen* had found the range, and, unlike the battleships, she could fire up to three rounds a minute. The likelihood was that the *Hood* would be hit again from one of her plunging 8in. shells, before she could close to within a safer range.

Then the *Bismarck* opened fire, and the salvo landed in the water close to the *Hood*. It was clear that, while the British gunnery was good, that of the Germans was even better. The second group of shell splashes was much larger than the first. It was now obvious the second ship was a battleship rather than a cruiser. Holland ordered Captain Kerr to switch targets, and ordered Captain Leach to do likewise, even though the *Prince of Wales* was already firing at *Bismarck*. He then addressed the problem of the angle of fire. At 5.55am he ordered a change of course to 280 degrees, which wasn't quite enough to bring his after guns into action. However, it would prevent the Germans from forcing their way past him into the Atlantic. As the range closed he would need to turn again, but for the moment his priority was to close the range as fast as possible. The range was now 22,000 yards (11 miles).

The *Hood* was still just inside its 'zone of invulnerability', and in fact the risk had just increased, as by heading towards the German ships at such an acute angle, the falling German shells had an 860ft-long (250m) target to hit, rather than a 105ft (32m) one if the *Hood* was beam on to the enemy. Owing to the way salvoes fell in a line along a single axis rather than being spread out, this increased the chances of the German shells hitting the target. On the course and speed he was on, Holland would be able to cross the 'T' of the German ships at about 6.10am, at close range. However, he also needed to change course to port to reduce the risk of being hit, and to clear the arc of fire of his aftermost guns. In effect it was the same problem facing Nelson at Trafalgar – to suffer enemy fire in order to close the range, or to turn to fire and lose the chance to strike a decisive blow.

THE *BISMARCK*'S FIFTH SALVO, BATTLE OF THE DENMARK STRAIT, 5.59AM, 24 MAY 1941 (pp.46–47)

After her lookouts sighted two British ships in the Denmark Straits the crew of the KMS Bismarck went to action stations. The battleship opened fire on the leading ship – HMS *Hood* – at 5.55am. Her FuMG 40G active radar **(1)** was malfunctioning, so fire control was by visual means only. Fortunately the sea was relatively calm, with a glassy swell and a light breeze – perfect conditions for optical rangefinders. *Bismarck* fired a salvo every minute – her third one at 5.57am bracketed the *Hood*, but didn't hit her. The two pairs of ships were on rapidly converging courses, which meant that the *Bismarck* was firing in her forward arc, the equivalent of 10 o'clock, with her after turrets trained round almost as far as they could bear **(2)**.

At 5.58am the *Bismarck* fired three salvoes in rapid succession – one every 30 seconds. This was her maximum rate of fire – according to German gunnery manuals these 38cm guns could fire their 800kg projectiles and reload again within 26 seconds. Her fifth salvo of the battle **(3)** was fired at 5.59am, at a range of 10 miles (19km). At that range it took the shells a full minute to reach their target. This was the salvo that caught the *Hood* as she was turning to port, and while most of the shells missed their target, one 15in. shell penetrated the quarterdeck of the *Hood*, just behind her aftermost turret. Observers on *Bismarck*'s bridge **(4)** were stunned to see the British battlecruiser blow up, with an immense sheet of flame followed by a dense cloud of yellow smoke. According to Oberleutnant zur See von Müllenheim-Rechberg, when the loudspeaker announced that 'The *Hood* is exploding', the crew stared at each other in disbelief. Then the shock passed, and they began celebrating. Ten miles (19km) away, 1,415 men had just lost their lives.

On the *Bismarck*, Lütjens was convinced that the second British ship was Vice Admiral Tovey's *King George V*, as the Germans were still unaware that the *Prince of Wales* had entered service. She was too important to leave alone, so he ordered the *Prinz Eugen* to switch targets to the British battleship, leaving the *Bismarck* to continue firing on the battlecruiser, which he now recognized as the *Hood*. The fire of the two German ships were now going to cross paths, so he also ordered Kapitän Brinkmann to reduce the speed of the *Prinz Eugen*, allowing the *Bismarck* to overtake her. The German cruiser would also be better placed to counter any moves made by the shadowing British cruisers, which up until now had taken no part in the action.

At 5.57am the *Prinz Eugen* switched her fire to the *Prince of Wales*, while the *Bismarck* fired at the *Hood*. This was the *Bismarck*'s third salvo. The second had fallen short, thwarted by Holland's change of course. The third salvo straddled the *Hood*, but didn't hit her. However, it was clear that the German battleship was now ranged in, and the next salvo might well score a hit or two. Since they first opened fire at 5.52am the British ships had each fired four salvoes from their forward facing guns, but had failed to score any hits. However, their shots were getting closer, and the next salvo from both ships might well straddle the German battleship. To help the gunners, at 5.59am Holland ordered another change of course – a 20-degree turn to port onto a new course of 260 degrees. At that angle the rear turrets of both British

An impression of the sinking of the *Hood*, first published in *Time Life* magazine. Both bow and stern sections rose up to form a huge 'V' shape before they sank. The *Prince of Wales* is shown racing past the wreckage.

ships would be able to fire on the *Bismarck*. The range was still decreasing steadily – it was now just over 18,000 yards (9 miles). In another minute the *Hood* would be out of her 'zone of vulnerability', and she would no longer be subject to plunging fire.

As the *Bismarck* had the range of the *Hood*, she fired three salvoes in quick succession, one every 30 seconds. The battlecruiser was just beginning her latest turn to port. The fourth salvo from the *Bismarck* landed half a minute later, straddling the *Hood* but scoring no hits. Her fifth salvo was fired at the same moment, and it arrived 30 seconds later, at 6am. Like the previous salvo, it straddled the target, but most of the shots fell harmlessly into the sea on the starboard side of the *Hood*. The Germans had decreased the range of their guns slightly, expecting their target to continue on her original course. The course change had taken them by surprise – the shells were aimed so that they would have landed on target if the *Hood* had maintained her old course. By the time the shells arrived only the battlecruiser's stern was still in the area covered by the fall of shot. It was enough.

One of the *Bismarck*'s 15in. shells struck the *Hood* in the stern, close to her after turrets. While we will never know exactly what happened. It seems that the *Bismarck*'s shell penetrated the vulnerable deck armour of the *Hood*, plunging through her decks into a magazine serving the after 4in. guns. The explosion created a flash flame that travelled to the engine room, where it rose through the vents and funnels to create a pillar of fire. It also ignited the magazine below 'X' turret, which blew the turret above it into the air, followed a split second later by 'Y' turret, which ripped the stern off the ship. Observers in the *Prince of Wales* saw this huge flame shoot up from abaft the *Hood*'s mainmast, followed immediately by an incredible explosion centred on the stern of the ship. A huge yellow cloud loomed over the stern of the battlecruiser, hiding the horror beneath.

Amazingly, on the bridge of the *Hood* nobody realized that their ship had been torn in two. The helmsman reported that the steering had gone, and an attempt was made to switch to emergency steering as the stricken hull began to capsize. A survivor stepped onto the starboard bridge wing and into the water. As he went he saw the admiral, still sitting in his command chair, as if resigned to the inevitable. The stern, 200ft (60m) long, tilted forwards and rose out of the water as its shattered compartments filled with water. The rest of the ship continued to slide through the water, propelled by momentum. The sixth salvo from the *Bismarck* landed at 6.01am, but missed the sinking ship. By that time the bow had slowed and stopped, and like the stern it too rose out of the water, as water flooded into it, and the forecastle slowly rose, before sliding beneath the surface of the water. In effect the wreckage formed a giant 'V'.

Three minutes after the fatal hit, the last traces of the Royal Navy's most famous ship had vanished, leaving a scattering of oil and wreckage, and three survivors out of her crew of 1,421 men. Both Vice Admiral Holland and Captain Kerr went down with their ship. On the *Prince of Wales*, a stunned Captain Leach had already begun his own turn to port, but he immediately ordered the battleship to be turned hard to starboard, to avoid colliding with the wreckage.

On all five remaining ships – three British and two German – those who witnessed the cataclysmic explosion recalled experiencing an immense shock, and were awed by the sheer scale of the destruction, and the loss of life. An observer on the *Bismarck* later claimed that the fireball seemed close enough to touch, and was followed by a shock wave which he likened to being in a hurricane. As a horrified Wake-Walker ordered the news to be radioed to the Admiralty, the stunned crew of the *Prince of Wales* were left to face the *Bismarck* and *Prinz Eugen* alone.

The last salvoes of the battle, photographed from *Prinz Eugen* at around 6.04am. The smoke on the left marks the location of the sinking *Hood*, while smoke and shell splashes to the right mark the location of *Prince of Wales*.

As Captain Leach resumed his original course he ordered his gunnery officer to target the *Bismarck*. After all, she was the most significant threat. Likewise, Kapitän Lindemann ordered his gunners to switch targets to the *Prince of Wales*. Fortunately for the German gunners, the battleship was now in roughly the same position as the *Hood* had been before she sank. *Prinz Eugen* was already firing at the British battleship, apart from the few minutes when the *Bismarck* blocked her line of fire as she overtook her. By 6.03am the range was down to 16,000 yards (8 miles).

A minute later a salvo from the *Prince of Wales* straddled the *Bismarck*, and scored a hit, which seemed to do no damage. Almost simultaneously the *Bismarck*'s first salvo against the new target straddled the *Prince of Wales*, and one shell struck her bridge. It didn't explode and passed on to land in the water, and Captain Leach was only stunned, but the bridge was turned into a charnel house. Apart from the captain, only two of the bridge staff survived. Control was temporarily switched to the aft control position, just as the *Prince of Wales* scored her first hit on the British battleship. Both German warships were now firing at the *Prince of Wales*, and scoring hits with almost every salvo.

One of these 8in. shells struck the fire-control director serving the secondary guns, while two more hit the battleship below the waterline, causing minor flooding. The only thing that spared Leach more damage was the slackening of fire as the *Bismarck* overtook the *Prinz Eugen*. By that time Captain Leach had resumed control of the battleship from his shattered bridge, and he ordered a hard turn to port, to prevent the range from closing any further. The two battleships were now 14,500 yards (7 miles) apart. By now though, the *Bismarck* was scoring some telling hits. Two 15in. shells hit the *Prince of Wales*, one amidships, next to her funnel, which started a major fire, and the other amidships on the waterline, a hit which didn't penetrate her belt, but caused some flooding and a fuel leak. In retaliation the *Prince of Wales* scored two more hits on the *Bismarck*, neither of which caused any major damage.

After just two minutes of this, at 6.05am, Captain Leach realized that the *Prince of Wales* was being outfought. Her radar had been knocked out, her Walrus spotter aircraft had been destroyed and her guns were starting to malfunction, despite everything the civilian contractors could do. 'X' turret had jammed owing to a hydraulic problem, which almost cut her firepower by half. Leach made the tough decision to break off the fight. He ordered the *Prince of Wales* to turn away onto a new course of 150 degrees, heading southeast, directly away from the *Bismarck*. He contacted Wake-Walker, who was now the senior officer in the area, and he agreed with Leach's decision.

Both German ships continued to fire, but the rapid change of course meant their salvoes missed their target. Four minutes later at 6.09am Leach ordered his men to make smoke to obscure the aim of the German gunners. At that point Lütjens ordered his two captains to cease fire. The battle of the Denmark Strait had lasted just 17 minutes, but in that short time almost 1,500 men had lost their lives, the British had lost the pride of their fleet, and Britain's most modern battleship had been outfought by her German counterpart.

When the order to cease fire was announced the crews of the two German ships cheered and celebrated their incredible victory. Lütjens was now free to roam through the Atlantic. All he needed to do now was to shake off Wake-Walker and his two irritatingly persistent British cruisers. Then the damage reports came in. At first it was thought that the *Prince of Wales*'s three hits had scored no real damage. Two had indeed caused minor structural damage, but the third had hit the *Bismarck* below the waterline, causing minor flooding, and more importantly a leak in a port fuel tank. Fuel was now seeping out into the Atlantic, and, while the battleship's crew worked to plug the leak and repair the damage, Lütjens wondered what impact the loss of fuel might have on his plans.

THE PURSUIT

Kapitän Lindemann wanted to pursue the *Prince of Wales* – he was convinced he could finish her off. Perhaps if Admiral Lütjens knew his enemy was indeed the *Prince of Wales*, with malfunctioning guns and a raw crew, he might well have agreed. Instead he vetoed the notion – after all, his orders were to avoid unnecessary engagements, and not to risk his ships any more than he had to. The two ships were already steering a course of 200 degrees, towards the south-south-west, and once again the *Prinz Eugen* took the lead,

The *Bismarck*, photographed from *Prinz Eugen* shortly after the battle of the Denmark Strait. She is down slightly by the bow, a result of flooding caused by a hit from a 14in. shell fired from the battleship *Prince of Wales*.

where her working radar could do the most good. By mid-morning it was clear that the *Bismarck* had lost a lot of fuel, and was down slightly by the bows. Lütjens realized that this would restrict her range of operations, and make an extensive cruise impossible. The *Bismarck* needed to be repaired before the operation could continue.

The nearest dry dock was at Saint-Nazaire in Brittany, on the French Atlantic coast. Saint-Nazaire was also close to Brest, where the *Scharnhorst* and *Gneisenau* were berthed. The damage to the *Bismarck* would take a week to repair, and then she would be ready for sea again, only this time she could be accompanied by the *Scharnhorst*. In other words, he planned to resurrect the original plan for Operation *Rheinübung*, uniting the most powerful ships in the Kriegsmarine into one powerful Seekampfgruppe. He also decided that the *Bismarck* would be better off operating on her own. He decided to detach the *Prinz Eugen*, allowing her to hunt independently before returning to the safety of the Baltic.

The damaged *Prince of Wales* had been joined by Wake-Walker and his cruisers, and the three British warships shadowed the German Seekampfgruppe as they steamed on into the Atlantic. Wake-Walker ordered the destroyers that had lagged behind Vice Admiral Holland's capital ships to scour the area where the *Hood* had sunk, in the hope of finding survivors. When the destroyer *Electra* arrived an hour after the sinking, she found a very dismal scene. One witness recalled how the crew expected to find hundreds of survivors. Instead they saw 'on the rolling swell, a large patch of oil ahead, a tangled pile of small wreckage… and that was all. Far over to starboard we saw three men – two of them swimming, one on a raft. But, in the chilling waters around them, there was no other sign of life.' The destroyers set course for Havelfjord, with their pitifully small group of survivors. On the British battleship damage control

The Home Fleet in all its majesty, photographed from the quarterdeck of *King George V* as it sailed to intercept the *Bismarck*. The battlecruiser *Repulse* is immediately astern of the flagship, while the aircraft carrier *Victorious* brings up the rear.

The *Bismarck* evades her pursuers

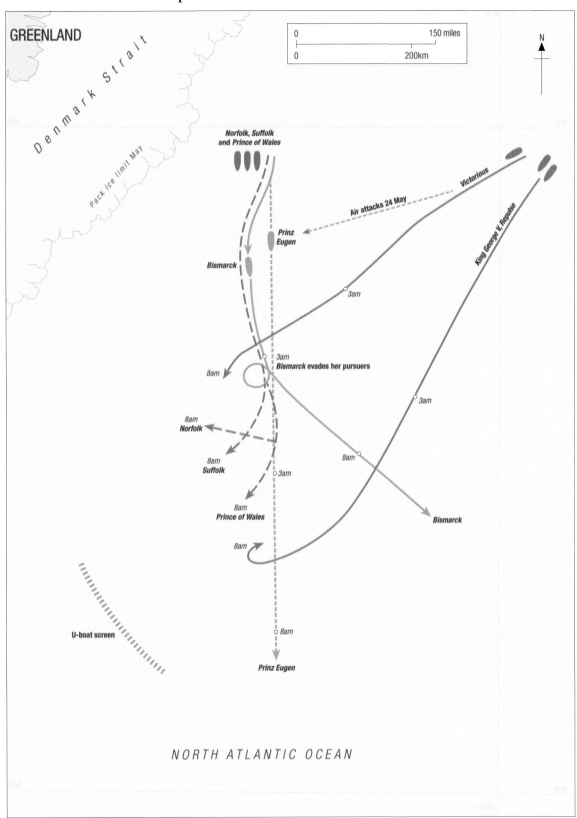

GREENLAND

Denmark Strait

Pack Ice limit May

Norfolk, Suffolk
and *Prince of Wales*

0   150 miles
0   200km

N

Air attacks 24 May

Victorious

King George V, Repulse

Prinz
Eugen

Bismarck

3am

3am
Bismarck evades her pursuers

8am

8am
Norfolk

3am

8am

8am
Suffolk

3am

8am

8am
Prince of Wales

Bismarck

8am

U-boat screen

8am

Prinz Eugen

NORTH ATLANTIC OCEAN

When the *Bismarck* broke out into the Atlantic the brand-new aircraft carrier *Victorious* was still 'working up', and her pilots lacked experience. Still, she was too useful an asset to leave behind, so Tovey ordered her to join the hunt.

parties and the poor civilian contractors worked through the morning to repair the main armament, so that by noon Captain Leach was confident he could renew the fight if need be.

The weather was clear, with only the occasional fog bank to obscure visibility, although conditions deteriorated slightly as the day wore on, and the fog thickened, until by early evening visibility had been reduced to around 6 miles (11km). Wake-Walker kept his distance from the Germans, but Lütjens knew he was being shadowed, and he did what he could to shake off his pursuers. He changed speed and course from time to time, but nothing seemed to work. Wake-Walker and Leach doggedly remained on his tail, sending Vice Admiral Tovey regular reports. That meant the British were gradually closing in.

When the Admiralty learned about the *Hood* disaster the First Sea Lord and his staff were shocked to the core, but they rallied and began to work out how best to pursue the *Bismarck*. The same was true in the warships of the Home Fleet – disbelief and shock was soon replaced by a desire for revenge. The dead had to be avenged, and the honour of the Royal Navy restored. The Admiralty – in consultation with Tovey – issued several immediate orders. First, the light cruisers *Manchester*, *Birmingham* and *Arethusa*, which

were still on patrol between Iceland and the Faeroes, were ordered to take up a new position in the Denmark Strait, forming a new screen there in case the *Bismarck* or the *Prinz Eugen* turned back towards Norway.

At 10.22am the powerful battleship *Rodney* and the destroyers *Somali*, *Tartar* and *Mashona* were detached from convoy escort duties, leaving the American-bound liner *Britannic* with a single destroyer as her escort. The *Rodney* was in bad shape, and desperately in need of a refit – the very reason she was sailing to the United States. Instead she was sent eastwards again, in an attempt to intercept the *Bismarck*.

The aged battleship *Ramillies* was detached from her eastbound convoy, and ordered to block the *Bismarck*'s path westward. The battleship *Revenge* in Halifax was ordered to sea, to help cover these scattered convoys. The cruisers *Edinburgh* and *Gloucester* were also at sea, patrolling the Atlantic. They were both ordered to steam towards the *Bismarck*. Finally, Vice Admiral Somerville's Force H based in Gibraltar was placed on stand-by for immediate operations in the mid-Atlantic. Somerville's group consisted of the aircraft carrier *Ark Royal*, the battlecruiser *Renown* and the light cruiser *Sheffield*.

A huddle of Swordfish torpedo bombers belonging to HMS *Victorious* ranged across the after end of her flight deck during air operations against the *Bismarck* on the afternoon of 23 May. These attacks by raw and inexperienced pilots proved unsuccessful.

This is the last photograph taken of the *Bismarck* from the *Prinz Eugen* before the cruiser parted company in the late afternoon of 23 May. *Bismarck* appears to be labouring slightly – the result of the flooding in her bow compartments.

Tovey in *King George V* was steaming towards the south-west, accompanied by *Victorious*, *Repulse* and Rear Admiral Curteis's 2nd Cruiser Squadron, which consisted of the light cruisers *Galatea*, *Aurora*, *Kenya* and *Neptune*. Nine destroyers also protected the force. At 2.40pm he sent the *Victorious* on ahead, escorted by the cruisers. By late afternoon Tovey expected the carrier to be within 80 miles (150km) of Lütjens – close enough to launch a strike.

Before Lütjens could detach the *Prinz Eugen*, he needed to shake off Wake-Walker. Therefore at 6.39pm the *Bismarck* made a sudden 180 degrees turn, her movement covered by a bank of fog. She emerged from it just 18,000 yards (9 miles) from the *Suffolk*, and opened fire on the British cruiser. After firing back the *Suffolk* turned away towards the north, taking advantage of the fog to confound the German gunners. This was exactly what Lütjens had hoped for. The *Prince of Wales* was 23,000 yards (11 miles) to the north, and both she and the *Norfolk* opened fire on the *Bismarck*. For a few minutes it looked like another full-scale battle would ensue. Two of the 14in. guns on the *Prince of Wales* malfunctioned again, and it was probably quite fortunate for Captain Leach that Lütjens had no intention of becoming embroiled in another battle.

Lütjens had already figured out that Wake-Walker was relying on the *Suffolk*'s radar. By driving her off he gained a small and temporary advantage – long enough to allow the *Prinz Eugen* to make her getaway. While the *Bismarck* engaged the British, Kapitän Brinkmann increased speed and raced off to the south, until she was beyond the range of the British radars. She then circled around Wake-Walker's ships before escaping to the north. With the *Prinz Eugen* safely detached Lütjens continued towards the south-west, and the long-range gunnery duel petered out. The German admiral knew that he had an ally out there in the gathering darkness.

A wolfpack of U-boats was operating somewhere ahead of him, in the mid-Atlantic. Lütjens hoped that with luck he could lure Wake-Walker towards the waiting U-boats. However, the Admiralty, who had intercepted their signals, had warned Wake-Walker about them. The British took every precaution that evening, but they also continued to shadow the *Bismarck* as she ran through the Atlantic night. At 8.56pm Lütjens radioed Berlin, to tell the Seekriegsleitung that he was heading towards Brest. That night it looked as if she would have a clear run into the French port. The only warship she encountered was a neutral one – the US Coastguard Ship *Modoc*, which was spotted just before midnight. The American sailors were able to watch the next phase of the drama unfold in front of them.

That evening, the *Victorious* approached the *Bismarck* from the west at 30 knots, her course dictated by Wake-Walker's reports. Just before 11pm Captain Bovell decided his carrier was just within range to launch a strike. He had nine Swordfish torpedo bombers ready, crewed by inexperienced pilots. There were being asked to take off at night, locate an enemy, attack her and return through the darkness to their ship. It was a challenge a veteran pilot would think twice about before accepting. These young air crews didn't hesitate. The nine Swordfish took off successfully, and led by Lieutenant-Commander Esmonde the lumbering biplanes headed south-west through the night. It was a miracle they located the *Bismarck*, but just after midnight they not only found her, but launched their attack, watched from a distance by the crew of the *Modoc*. In fact, the Swordfish began their run against the American ship, before realizing that the *Bismarck* lay further ahead.

The *Bismarck* began to zigzag, and her gun crews were ready. A wall of flak began erupting from her anti-aircraft guns. It was difficult enough to hit a fast-moving zigzagging battleship with a plane-launched torpedo in the semi-dark. It was especially difficult from a Swordfish, which had to make a seemingly suicidal run towards the target at less than 100ft (33m), and at a speed of less than 90 knots. The biplanes seemed like easy targets, but in fact the *Bismarck*'s modern gunnery directors had trouble dealing with a foe that approached so slowly, and most of the flak burst ahead of the oncoming planes. Amazingly all the planes survived the attack, but one was hit, and only one of their torpedoes hit their target. It struck the *Bismarck* amidships on her starboard side, causing minor flooding, but inflicting no real damage. The flooding temporarily reduced her speed to 16 knots, but within an hour she was forging ahead again, as if nothing had happened. By a miracle, all of the Swordfish made it back to *Victorious*, where their exhausted crews must have been delighted to have survived their ordeal.

The pursuit continued. At midnight the Admiralty ordered Vice Admiral Somerville to set sail from Gibraltar, as it hoped to trap the *Bismarck* between the pincers of Tovey's Home Fleet and Somerville's Force H. There was still a chance that the *King George V* and *Repulse* could overhaul the *Bismarck* during the night, as long as Wake-Walker's signals kept reporting her position. Force H was an added insurance, in case the two forces missed each other.

Flying Officer Dennis Briggs of Coastal Command piloted the Catalina flying boat that relocated the elusive *Bismarck* during the morning of 26 May, ending 24 hours of uncertainty. In this photograph he is recounting the tale during a radio interview.

Vice Admiral Somerville's Force H at sea. In the foreground is Somerville's flagship, the battlecruiser *Renown*. Behind her is the aircraft carrier *Ark Royal*, with Swordfish ranged at the after end of her flight deck, and then the light cruiser *Sheffield*.

To keep up the pressure, at 1.30am the *Prince of Wales* opened fire on the *Bismarck* from 20,000 yards (10 miles) astern of her, but visibility deteriorated, and the brief action was broken off. Instead it was left up to the *Suffolk* to maintain contact with her radar, with Wake-Walker's keeping a safe distance 25,000 yards (12 miles) behind and slightly to the east of the *Bismarck*. The only complication was the threat posed by those U-boats, and Wake-Walker gave orders for his three ships to begin zigzag manoeuvres, just in case a U-boat was lying in wait for them in the darkness. That gave Admiral Lütjens an opportunity – all he needed was luck and a great sense of timing.

Lütjens had his lookouts follow the British manoeuvres, and he bided his time. Then, shortly before 3am *Suffolk* 'zagged' towards the south-east, having just 'zigged' along a south-westerly course. It was the moment Lütjens had been waiting for. He had been making less than 20 knots, but he suddenly increased speed, and made a hard turn to starboard, which meant he was steaming directly away from *Suffolk*, and out of radar range. *Suffolk* lost contact at 3.06am, by which time *Bismarck* was heading westwards at full speed. When the *Suffolk* turned again she was unable to relocate the *Bismarck*. Wake-Walker ordered his ships to increase speed and fan out to the south-west, hoping to regain contact. Lütjens had been expecting that, and instead he looped round to the north-west and then the north, finally crossing the path of the British force some 20 miles (37km) astern of Wake-Walker's ships – well outside radar range. Then, the *Bismarck* settled onto a south-easterly course of 130 degrees and quietly steamed through the night, heading towards the French coast. Lütjens had outfoxed the British again, who now had no idea where the *Bismarck* might be.

For the British, losing contact with the *Bismarck* was a calamity. When Captain Ellis of the *Suffolk* reported the news at 3.15am, Wake-Walker didn't tell Tovey immediately, and so *King George V* and *Repulse* continued on their original course towards the south-west, as Tovey hoped to be in a position to intercept the *Bismarck* around 9am on the morning of 25 May. Wake-Walker preferred to carry out his own fruitless search of the area. When the report was passed on to Tovey at around 6am, he ordered Captain Leach to join him in *Prince of Wales*, leaving Wake-Walker's two cruisers to continue the search. At 8am Tovey was approaching the area where he expected to have intercepted the *Bismarck*, but by that time the German battleship was 150 miles (280km) away to the north-east, crossing Tovey's track at right angles. At dawn *Victorious* launched its Swordfish again, conducting an unsuccessful aerial search of the area to the north-west of Wake-Walker's cruisers. It seemed as if the *Bismarck* had vanished into thin air. Worse, it would be almost 24 hours before the British had any firm news of her.

It was an extremely tense period, and while Tovey and his superiors in the Admiralty tried to guess where Lütjens might be heading, warships and search aircraft combed the North Atlantic, searching for the elusive battleship. Strangely enough the *Prinz Eugen* had also sailed right past Tovey as well. After evading pursuit she turned south. At dawn she was about 150 miles (280km) south of Tovey's main force, well out of the area in which the British were searching. Tovey considered Lütjens' possible moves. If the *Bismarck* had been damaged in the battle of the Denmark Strait, she might try to return to Norway, or towards the French coast.

A Swordfish torpedo bomber, pictured flying over the aircraft carrier *Ark Royal*. She carried more aircraft than *Victorious*, but the strike aircraft she did carry were still obsolete Swordfish, whose short range and slow speed made them of limited effectiveness.

Searching for the *Bismarck*

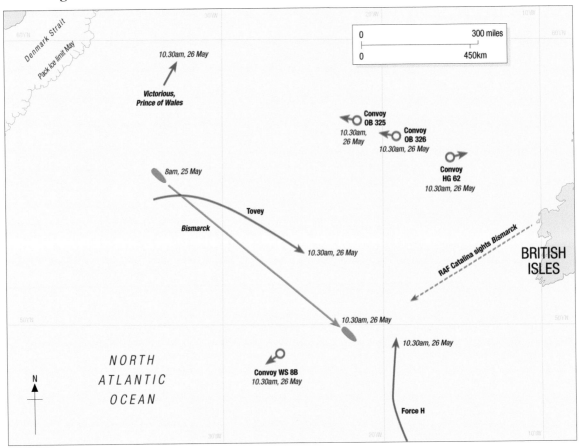

If the *Bismarck* was not damaged then Lütjens could be anywhere, but more than likely he would still be operating somewhere in the North Atlantic, astride the convoy routes between Britain and Newfoundland. The great fear was that the *Bismarck* would be able to rendezvous with a German tanker, which would increase her operational range. As the Admiralty had sent every available British battleship to sea, all Lütjens had to do was to wait for a few days until lack of fuel forced them back into port. He would then be free to strike at will.

Fuel was already becoming a real problem. At noon on 25 May Wake-Walker's cruisers had to break off their search and return to Havelfjord to refuel. After refuelling, *Suffolk* was ordered to guard the Denmark Strait while Wake-Walker in *Norfolk* was ordered south to join Tovey. The *Victorious* was also running short of fuel, and later that afternoon she returned to Scapa Flow, leaving Tovey without an aircraft carrier until *Ark Royal* arrived from Gibraltar. *Repulse* headed to Newfoundland for the same reason, and by nightfall the *Prince of Wales* was forced to head north to Havelfjord, leaving Tovey to continue the search with *King George V* and a handful of destroyers.

That means that when he needed it most in the 24 hours after the *Bismarck* broke contact, Tovey was stripped of almost all of his most powerful warships. Tovey lacked the resources to search everywhere, so he decided to concentrate his search to the south-west, where the *Bismarck*

Closing in on the prey

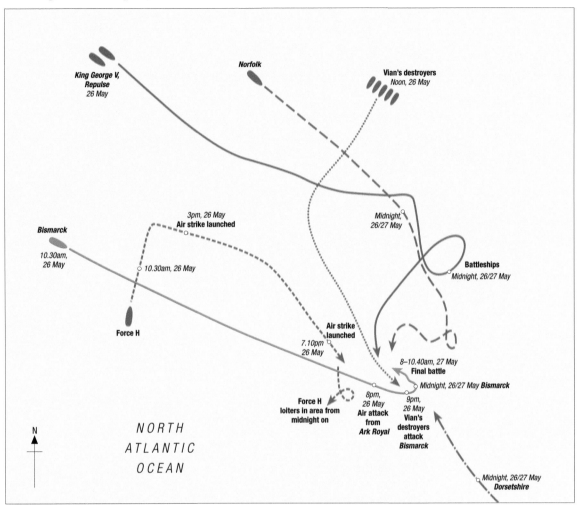

King George V, Repulse
26 May

Norfolk

Vian's destroyers
Noon, 26 May

3pm, 26 May
Air strike launched

Midnight,
26/27 May

Bismarck

10.30am,
26 May

10.30am, 26 May

Battleships
Midnight, 26/27 May

Force H

Air strike
launched

7.10pm
26 May

8–10.40am, 27 May
Final battle

Midnight, 26/27 May Bismarck

Force H
loiters in area from
midnight on

8pm,
26 May
Air attack
from
Ark Royal

9pm,
26 May
Vian's
destroyers
attack
Bismarck

N

NORTH
ATLANTIC
OCEAN

Midnight, 26/27 May
Dorsetshire

would pose the greatest threat to British convoys. Although other units, including Force H, were approaching the naval arena, he still had an awful lot of ocean to cover, and all too few ships and aircraft to search with.

Fortunately, help was at hand. Captain Dalrymple-Hamilton's battleship *Rodney* and her escort of three destroyers was a few hundred miles to the east, and, having detached herself from her close escort of the liner *Britannic*, she was sailing west to join Tovey at dawn on 26 May. *Ramillies* was still off Newfoundland, too far away to intervene, but the County-class cruiser *Dorsetshire* was also heading north after having been detached from Convoy SL74, which was to the west of the Azores. Away to the south-east, Somerville's Force H was steaming north-north-west, and would reached a position in the Western Approaches some 350 miles (650km) to the west of Brest by the morning of 26 May. No fewer than seven convoys were at sea in the North Atlantic though, and the *Bismarck* might attack any of them sometime during that long nerve-wracking day. By the time darkness fell late on the evening of 25 May, the *Bismarck* had still not been spotted. While this was good news for the convoys, it did little for Tovey's peace of mind.

HMS *Sheffield*, the 6in. light cruiser attached to Force H. On 26 May she was shadowing *Bismarck* when she was attacked by Swordfish from *Ark Royal*, but fortunately the leading airmen missed their target, and the rest aborted the attack.

However, by then he had a better idea where the *Bismarck* might be. At around 10am that morning a German warship had transmitted a long radio signal in code. It was the *Bismarck*, informing the Seekriegsleitung about the battle of the Denmark Strait, and outlining the damage suffered by the *Bismarck* during the short battle. The fact that Lütjens broke radio silence suggests that he still thought the British were shadowing him. Evidently he was unaware that he had evaded his pursuers. Inevitably, the British intercepted the message, and, after triangulating it, the Admiralty were able to conclude that the *Bismarck* lay to the south-east of Tovey, although Tovey's own intelligence officers placed the source more to the east. In any event it gave him a better idea of where the *Bismarck* was, and where she might be heading. If Lütjens had maintained radio silence then the outcome of the campaign might have been very different indeed.

Tovey duly turned his flagship around, and headed east, and all the other converging British ships altered course accordingly. Tovey now suspected that the *Bismarck* might be heading towards a French port. After all, the radio message placed a great emphasis on the damage suffered by the battleship. That meant she was steaming towards Saint-Nazaire or Brest. The hunt for the *Bismarck* had now become a pursuit, with both the Home Fleet and Force H heading towards the same approximate point, some 250 miles (460km) to the south-west of Ireland. It also meant that for the first time Tovey knew roughly where to look.

Soon after dawn on the morning of Monday 26 May, two Catalina flying boats took off from the Coastal Command base at Loch Erne in Northern Ireland and headed south-west. Visibility was poor. Just after 10.25am Lieutenant Briggs piloting one of the Catalinas spotted a large ship in the distance. He knew that a British capital ship would have a destroyer escort surrounding her, to protect her from U-boats. Briggs dropped down for a closer look, and almost immediately he was fired on by anti-aircraft guns, which damaged the Catalina. Only one enemy warship could have carried all that firepower. Briggs evaded the enemy fire, while his radio operator sent the news back to Coastal Command. Some 31 hours since the British lost contact, and 24 hours since Lütjens broke radio silence, the *Bismarck* had finally been spotted.

She was heading on a south-westerly course at 20 knots – Lütjens had been keeping his speed down to save fuel. Within an hour news of the sighting had reached Vice Admiral Tovey on board *King George V*. A quick glance at the plotting table showed him that Lütjens was winning the race. She was too far away for the *King George V* or *Rodney* to intercept the *Bismarck*. Only Somerville's Force H was close enough to overhaul her, as it was then 150 miles (280km) to the east, between the *Bismarck* and the French ports. To the north Captain Vian was also trying to intercept the Bismarck with his flotilla of five destroyers, but he was too far way to block the Bismarck's progress. Only Force H was in the right place. Somerville knew that the *Renown* was too poorly armed to hold her own in a duel with the *Bismarck*. His main offensive weapon was the *Ark Royal* with her Swordfish torpedo bombers.

When confirmation of the *Bismarck*'s position reached Somerville at noon, he had already crossed Bismarck's path and was to the north of her. He immediately ordered his three ships – *Ark Royal*, *Renown* and *Sheffield* – to turn onto a course of 120 degrees, which was parallel to the course steered by the Bismarck and 120 miles (220km) to the north. At 1.15pm Somerville ordered *Sheffield* to steer a course of 145 degrees in an attempt to pick up *Bismarck* on her radar. Meanwhile, the air crews of *Ark Royal* were preparing to launch a strike.

At 3pm a force of 15 Swordfish torpedo-bombers took off from *Ark Royal*, and headed south-south-east towards the enemy battleship. Unfortunately, during their briefing nobody told them that *Sheffield* now lay between them and their quarry, some 25,000 yards (12 miles) off the *Bismarck*'s port quarter. At 4.10pm the leading flight of Swordfish spotted their target, and they began their torpedo run. They were attacking the wrong ship. The captain of the *Sheffield* ordered his men to hold their fire, while he took drastic evasive action, throwing his cruiser to port to avoid the oncoming torpedoes.

A flight of Swordfish torpedo bombers, each carrying a single 18in. Mark XII aerial torpedo. These planes had a top speed of just over 100mph (160km/h), and were considered obsolete, but they remained in service as no better replacement was available.

THE AIR STRIKES FROM THE *ARK ROYAL*, 26 MAY 1941 (48° NORTH, 20° WEST)

By the afternoon of 26 May it was apparent that the only way the *Bismarck* could be prevented from reaching Brest was by launching an airstrike from HMS *Ark Royal*. The aircraft carrier was part of Vice Admiral Somerville's Force H, which was then to the north of *Bismarck*. Somerville sent the light cruiser *Sheffield* to establish radar contact with the German battleship, while the aircrews of the Ark Royal prepared the first of two strikes against *Bismarck*. This would be the Royal Navy's last chance to stop her, so the stakes were incredibly high.

BRITISH FORCES
1   *Ark Royal*
2   *Renown*
3   *Sheffield*
4   First Swordfish strike
5   Second Swordfish strike

GERMAN FORCES
A   *Bismarck*

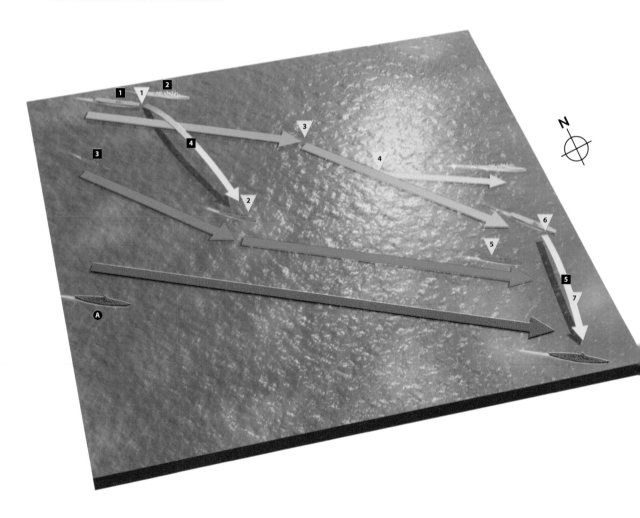

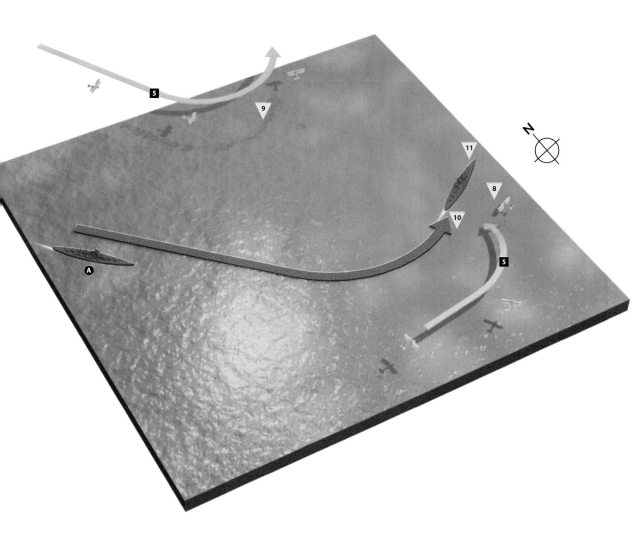

▼ EVENTS

1 3pm: first air strike launched from *Ark Royal*, consisting of 15 Swordfish torpedo bombers. The aircrews weren't told that *Sheffield* would be in the area.

2 4.10pm: *Sheffield* attacked in a 'friendly fire' incident. Fortunately faulty torpedoes prevented any damage being inflicted, and the air strike returned to the *Ark Royal*. The aircraft were rearmed.

3 5.20pm: Somerville alters course to place *Ark Royal* closer to *Bismarck*. He realizes that if another strike is to be launched he has to shorten the range between *Ark Royal* and the *Bismarck*.

4 6.05pm: Somerville in *Renown* alters course to maintain distance from *Bismarck*, while *Ark Royal* edges closer to launch her strike.

5 6.30pm: *Sheffield* shadows *Bismarck*, at extreme radar range, and reports changes of course and speed. The *Bismarck* continues her high-speed run towards Brest. There was just time to launch one more strike before nightfall.

6 7.10pm: Second air strike launched from *Ark Royal*. The two ships were now 100 miles apart.

7 8.47pm: *Bismarck* sighted by the aircraft. The strike leader Lt. Cdr. Coode planned to launch coordinated attacks, with his five flights approaching the target from different angles. Instead, the flights were separated by thick cloud, and so the attacks were launched in a piecemeal fashion.

8 Two aircraft attacked from the *Bismarck*'s starboard beam. The planes were damaged, but no hits were scored.

9 Four more attacked simultaneously from the port side, and at least one ineffective hit might have been scored. German fire was accurate – one Swordfish was hit 175 times, but all planes returned home safely.

10 The remaining aircraft attack simultaneously from the port and starboard beam. At 9.05pm a single torpedo hits her rudder in her rudder and after steering compartment. The attack completed, the Swordfish return to *Ark Royal*.

11 9.30pm: *Sheffield* reports that *Bismarck* steering an erratic course. It becomes evident that the German battleship has been damaged.

Dropping an aerial torpedo from a Swordfish was a tricky business. First the aircraft had to lead the target to compensate for the running time, then drop it from less than 100ft (30m), at a speed of around 100 knots.

Fortunately they missed, while others exploded on contact with the water owing to a problem with their magnetic detonators. The second wave realized the mistake, and the attack was aborted. While the sheepish air crews returned to their carrier, the *Bismarck* continued on her way.

The planes were refuelled and re-armed, and the faulty magnetic detonators replaced with a more reliable contact variety. Meanwhile the afternoon was turning into evening. After dusk, the chance of attacking and damaging the *Bismarck* would be minimal. This meant that there was barely time to launch one more air strike before *Bismarck* was protected by the darkness. Even then, the chances of inflicting a telling hit were considered remote. Still, it was the only chance the British now had of stopping the battleship.

On the *Bismarck*, Lütjens realized that a carrier was within range as he was being shadowed by a reconnaissance Swordfish. However, as the hours passed and evening approached he must have thought that the British had missed their chance. He was still doing 20 knots – his speed limited by the shortage of fuel – but he was still on course to reach Saint-Nazaire. The following morning the *Bismarck* would be within air range of the French coast, and Lütjens knew the Luftwaffe were planning to protect his ship with a fighter screen dense enough to deter any British attack. Darkness meant safety.

At 7.10pm, a second strike took off from *Ark Royal*, 100 miles (185km) to the north-west of the *Bismarck*'s position. When his first strike returned Somerville had ordered his carrier to move on a converging course with Lütjens to reduce the flying time needed to reach the target. He realized that every minute of daylight might be crucial. The three flights of Swordfish lost sight of each other in the low cloud, but the leading flight spotted the *Sheffield*, and helped vector in the remaining flights towards the target. They approached the *Bismarck* from a south-easterly course, and, at 8.40pm, they spotted the enemy battleship.

The first flight began its attack at 8.47pm. The other two flights followed over the next 20–30 minutes, after circling round the battleship to hit her from both sides at the same time. The *Bismarck*'s gunners opened up with an intense anti-aircraft barrage, but the slow-moving Swordfish proved difficult targets for the integrated anti-aircraft systems of the German battleship,

A Swordfish torpedo bomber, returning to the aircraft carrier *Ark Royal* after launching an abortive strike against the *Bismarck* during the afternoon of 26 May. This attack resulted in a 'friendly fire incident' when the airmen mistook *Sheffield* for the *Bismarck*.

AIR ATTACK BY SWORDFISH FROM HMS *ARK ROYAL*, 9.10PM, 26 MAY 1941 (pp.70–71)

By the afternoon of 26 May it was clear that the only chance of stopping *Bismarck* was to launch an air attack from the *Ark Royal*. The first strike launched failed to locate the target, and by the time the aircraft were readied again there was time for only one more attempt before dark. At 7.10am a strike of 15 Swordfish torpedo bombers took off from *Ark Royal* – three flights of five biplanes apiece.

The flights became separated by cloud, and as a result attacks were uncoordinated, launched in twos and threes over a period of 20–30 minutes, torpedo runs being made on both the port and the starboard side of the *Bismarck*. There is still some confusion over which aircraft actually launched the torpedo that hit her stern. One pilot, Lieutenant Owen-Smith, saw a column of water rise over her stern on her starboard side, although the decisive hit is often credited to Sub-Lieutenant

Moffat, who attacked from port. Therefore, the honour might well go to Lieutenant Godfrey-Faussett of 810 Squadron. He launched his Mark XIII torpedo at a range of approximately 800 yards **(1)**, and at a height of around 50ft (15m) from the water. He was aiming at a point roughly two ship lengths ahead of the target **(2)** – the distance *Bismarck* was expected to travel during the 70 seconds the torpedo would take to reach her. As soon as the torpedo was released the aircraft turned away – one of the reasons why the identity of the successful aircraft remains unclear. Fortunately the slow speed of the Swordfish helped to confuse the German gunners, so most of the flak burst ahead or above the aircraft. Godfrey-Faussett managed to make good his escape, and return to his ship, unaware that he or one of his fellow airmen had managed to cripple the German battleship.

designed to counter much speedier enemy planes. Out of the first wave of five planes three, or possibly four torpedoes missed. One hit was scored amidships on the port side by the first wave, and a possible second torpedo may have struck the same spot moments after the first. However, no serious damage was caused, as the torpedoes struck the *Bismarck*'s thick armoured belt. All the torpedoes from the second flight missed their target. That left one last flight of five antiquated Swordfish.

Three of this last flight attacked from port, and the remaining two approached the battleship from starboard. Four of them missed. The other was fired a textbook two ship-lengths ahead of the *Bismarck*, at a range of approximately 800 yards (730m). Just as he had done several times before, Kapitän Lindemann ordered a hard turn to port, trying to miss the oncoming torpedo. If she had remained on course the torpedo would have struck the *Bismarck* amidships, on her impervious armoured belt. Instead the torpedo struck her stern, jamming her rudder as it was angled 15 degrees to port. Water flooded into the battleship's steering compartment, making it hard for the damage-control teams to asses the damage.

Viewed from a British reconnaissance plane, the erratic track of the *Bismarck* can be seen in this remarkable photograph, taken soon after dawn on 27 May. Within an hour the German battleship would go into action for the last time.

Captain Philip Vian DSO already had a formidable reputation as a destroyer commander before he launched his flotilla in a night-time attack on the *Bismarck*. His aggressive performance denied the Germans any respite before their final battle the following morning.

As dusk fell the last Swordfish flew off towards the north-west, leaving the *Bismarck* still lazily turning to port. When the damage-control parties managed to examine the rudder, they found that there was little they could do. The rudder could be repaired only in port. Lindemann did what he could to counteract the effect of the jammed rudders, but he was only partially successful. That one last torpedo hit had forced the *Bismarck* from her course, and sealed her fate.

As the aircraft returned to *Ark Royal* the air crews felt they had failed, until a signal from *Sheffield* reported that the *Bismarck* was steering erratically, and was circling around to the north-west, heading away from safety. As the air crews were debriefed it suddenly made sense – the last torpedo hit had somehow prevented the *Bismarck* from steering a course towards the French coast. This meant that at last Tovey's battleships had a chance to overhaul her and bring the damaged German warship to battle.

Tovey could just reach her during the hours of darkness, but he decided against a night action. His battleships were short of fuel, and bringing on a night-time battle would mean increasing their speed, which would mean they would have to break away to refuel soon after dawn. Delaying the battle until dawn would allow Tovey to place his ships in a better position, and by sailing through the night at a more economical speed his battleships would have almost two hours to deal with the *Bismarck*, before they had to break off and head for Scapa Flow.

Just before 10.40pm five destroyers of Captain Philip Vian's 4th Destroyer Flotilla took up station around the *Bismarck*, forming up with two destroyers on each beam, and the fifth one astern of her. The Germans opened fire on the destroyers to starboard – HMS *Maori* and the Polish destroyer *Piorun*, and Vian ordered his captains to pull back out of range. Vian was only biding his time, and at 11.24pm he ordered them to close in again, this time to launch a torpedo attack from several directions at once. However, poor visibility and the accuracy of the German fire forced him to abandon this near-suicidal torpedo attack. The destroyers withdrew again, but Vian gave his captains permission to attack on their own initiative if the opportunity presented itself.

Zulu was the first to attack from port at 1.20am. All four of her torpedoes missed, the aimers hampered by rain squalls and accurate German gunfire. *Maori* was next, attacking from starboard, but she too failed to score any hits. Next it was the turn of Vian's flagship *Cossack*, followed by *Sikh*. Both destroyers claimed to score one hit apiece, but German survivors do not support this claim. They may well have seen flashes from starshells through the rain-laden darkness, and assumed they were caused by explosions. Also, *Bismarck* stopped in the water for an hour, from 1.48am. This wasn't because of damage, but to allow Lindemann's damage-control parties to examine the rudder. Within an hour the *Bismarck* was under way again. Vian's attacks had failed, but he had kept the Germans at their posts through the night.

On the *Bismarck* the crew were finally beginning to realize that their chances of reaching safety had evaporated. Saint-Nazaire was still 500 miles (925km) away, and when dawn came there would be no German aircraft, as they were still out of range of air cover. Instead, they could expect the British Home Fleet. Although *Bismarck* could still fight, the damage to her rudder meant that she was unable to avoid an engagement against superior enemy forces. In other words, her luck had run out.

HMS *Maori* (F-24) was one of Captain Vian's Tribal-class destroyers that harassed the *Bismarck* during the evening of 26 May. Each carried four 21in. torpedoes, and she and her companions launched them at the *Bismarck* under cover of darkness.

Just before midnight Lütjens radioed the Seekreigsleitung, telling them that he was unable to reach the French coast. He ended with the words 'We fight to the last in our belief in you, my Führer, and in the firm faith of Germany's victory'. In Kiel, Großadmiral Raeder ordered U-boats to provide what help they could, but it was a largely empty gesture. Although the signals continued throughout the night, everyone now realized that the *Bismarck* was on her own. Her young and exhausted crew could do little else but wait for dawn, and the arrival of a British battle fleet eager for revenge.

This bow view of HMS *Rodney* highlights her ungainly appearance. Still, like her sister ship HMS *Nelson* pictured behind her, her design was extremely practical, and her nine 16in. guns provided her with significantly greater firepower than her German adversary.

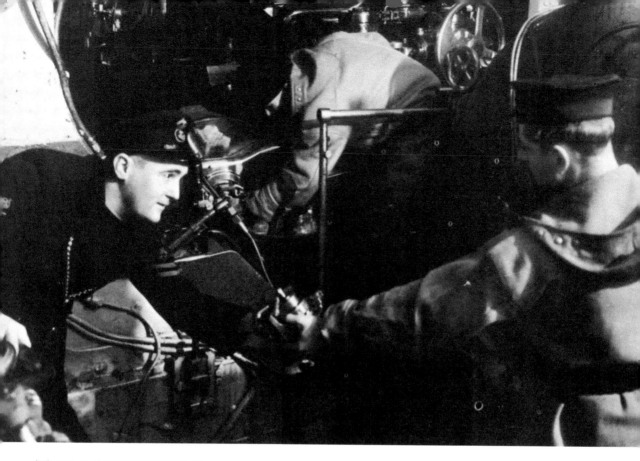

THE LAST BATTLE

As dawn broke on 27 May, both sides braced themselves for the coming battle. Vice Admiral Tovey was approaching the *Bismarck* from the west, which meant the German battleship would be silhouetted by the early morning sun. Late the previous evening Rear Admiral Wake-Walker had arrived in *Norfolk*, having refuelled in Iceland. Tovey sent the cruiser on ahead, to help guide the battleships towards their target. Lookouts on *Norfolk* spotted the familiar silhouette of *Bismarck* at 7.53am, and Wake-Walker immediately radioed the news to Tovey. He also took command of Vian's destroyers, down to four as an hour before the *Piorun* had to break off and return to Plymouth to refuel. The destroyers were still stationed around the German battleship, but were keeping their distance. The *Bismarck* was heading in a roughly northerly direction, making 10 knots.

Soon after 8am Tovey arrived in *King George V*, coming in sight astern of *Norfolk*. The *Rodney* was still a few miles astern of him, and Tovey ordered the captains of the two battleships to attack from different directions, in order to split the *Bismarck*'s fire. While he knew that the mighty German warship was unable to evade him, he also realized that her armament was still intact, and she could still cause serious damage to either of the British capital ships. Tovey planned to use his advantage of manoeuvrability to dictate the course and timing of the coming battle. Somerville in *Renown* was a good 30,000 yards (15 miles) to the south of the *Bismarck*, with *Ark Royal* and *Sheffield*, and would take no part in the coming battle. It was up to Tovey to finish off the wounded enemy battleship. He and his men were eager to avenge the *Hood*.

HMS *Rodney* had the firepower to cripple the *Bismarck*, if only the ageing battleship could catch up with her. Her 16in. guns were mounted in three triple turrets, where the crews seen here were to assist the mechanical loaders.

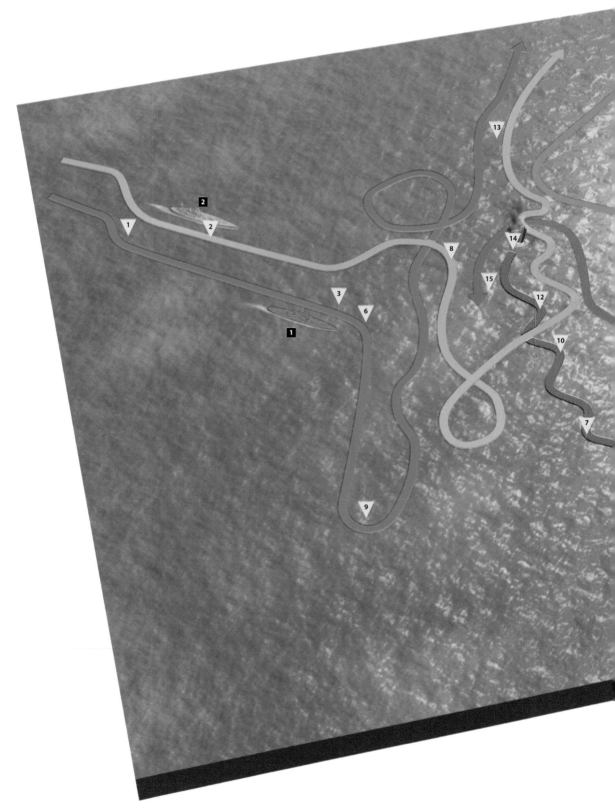

BRITISH FORCES
1 *King George V*
2 *Rodney*
3 *Norfolk*
4 *Dorsetshire*

GERMAN FORCES
A *Bismarck*

▼ EVENTS

1 8.45am: *Bismarck* sighted by *King George V* and *Rodney*. *Rodney* turns to port, to widen the gap between her and the flagship.

2 8.47am: *Rodney* opens fire at a range of 11.5 miles. *Bismarck* returns fire a minute later. Her initial shooting is highly accurate.

3 8.48am: *King George V* opens fire. Her initial accuracy is hindered by radar rangefinding problems, and shell splashes around the target from *Rodney's* shells.

4 8.54am: *Norfolk* opens fire. Her 8in. shells add to the maelstrom of shell splashes surrounding the German battleship.

5 8.59am: *Bismarck* hit by a 16in. shell from *Rodney*, knocking out her main fire-control director.

6 8.59am: *King George V* alters course to starboard, to split the enemy fire.

7 9.02am: The *Bismarck* is hit repeatedly. 'Anton' and 'Bruno' turrets are put out of action. Fires are now raging on the decks of the German battleship.

8 9.15am: *Rodney* alters course to starboard, to ensure all her guns can hit the target. The range is now down to just 6 miles.

9 9.16am: *King George V* turns towards the north, as her guns were moving out of their arc of fire.

10 9.30am: *Bismarck's* guns silenced. She is now blazing fiercely.

11 9.40am: *Dorsetshire* opens fire. Her 8in. shells begin adding to the repeated hits being scored by *King George V*, *Rodney* and *Norfolk*.

12 It is becoming clear the *Bismarck* will require underwater hits to sink her.

13 10.15am: Tovey orders his battleships to break off the engagement. He will rely on torpedoes from *Dorsetshire* to finish off the shattered enemy warship.

14 10.15am: On *Bismarck*, orders given to abandon ship. Fires are now raging from stem to stern, and hundreds of survivors attempt to escape into the sea.

15 10.30am: *Dorsetshire* finishes off *Bismarck* with torpedoes. The *Bismarck* finally sinks at 10.40am.

THE *BISMARCK'S* LAST BATTLE, 27 MAY 1941 (48° 10' NORTH, 16° 15' WEST)

The final act of the drama played out soon after dawn on the morning of 27 May. The British admiral decided to attack the stricken German battleship from the west, which meant that the *Bismarck* would be silhouetted clearly against the early morning sun. The *Bismarck* might have been unable to manoeuvre, but her guns were still fully operational, and she was still capable of damaging or driving off Tovey's two battleships.

At 8.45am, lookouts on the *King George V* spotted the *Bismarck* 25,000 yards (12 miles) away to the south-east. She was still steering an erratic northerly course. *Rodney* altered course slightly to port, to widen the distance between her and the flagship. She opened fire with her two forward 16in. turrets at 8.47am, followed a minute later by the 14in. forward turrets of Tovey's flagship. Three minutes later *Bismarck* fired back, aiming at *Rodney*; Lütjens presumed the *King George V* was the same battleship he had damaged in the Denmark Strait, making her less of a threat than *Rodney*. He was completely unaware that both British battleships were new opponents, and completely undamaged. Lindemann used his engines to turn the *Bismarck* slightly to starboard, so that all of her four turrets could bear on the *Rodney*.

The *Bismarck*'s gunnery was impressive – the *Rodney* was straddled with her third salvo. However, two battleships were now firing at her, and at 8.54am they were joined by *Norfolk*, with her 8in. guns added to the maelstrom of shell splashes surrounding the German ship. At 8.59am *Rodney* scored a telling hit at a range of 22,000 yards (11 miles), knocking out the *Bismarck*'s main gun director. That hit significantly reduced the risk of the *Bismarck*'s shells hitting the *Rodney*. It would take time for her to switch over to her after fire control director, and even then accuracy would still be reduced.

At the same moment – 8.59am, the *King George V* altered course to starboard, to allow her rear turret to fire. Given the angle of approach to the *Bismarck*, *Rodney* had now 'cleared her arcs' too by also turning to starboard, meaning that both British battleships could now engage the *Bismarck* with all their main guns. The range had now dropped to 21,000 yards (10 miles). Lindemann responded by turning away to starboard slightly, and shifting targets to the *King George V*, which was better served by the aft director. However, both British battleships were now straddling their target, which mean that further hits were almost inevitable.

Shell salvoes from *King George V* and *Rodney* – marked by the white plumes of spray – fall astern of the *Bismarck* during her final battle. Within minutes the shells would find their mark, and pound the cornered German vessel without remorse.

At 9.02am one of *Rodney's* 16in. shells struck *Bismarck*'s 'Bruno' turret, penetrating its armour and knocking it out of action. The blast also temporarily silenced the guns of 'Anton' turret too, and it was a good 25 minutes before they would fire again, with one final salvo. The *Bismarck* was still firing back with her after turrets, and four salvoes from them landed uncomfortably close to Tovey's flagship. Then, at around 9.15am a 14in. shell

from *King George V* knocked the *Bismarck*'s after gun director out of action. That meant that her two remaining turrets could continue to fire only under local control, the guns aimed and pointed by the turret crews themselves. By this time the heavy cruiser *Dorsetshire* had arrived from the south, and her 8in. shells began to range in on the now hopelessly outgunned German warship.

At that time both British battleships were heading south. The *Bismarck* was to the east, about 12,000 yards (6 miles) on their port beam, and heading in the opposite direction. *Norfolk* and *Dorsetshire* were a similar distance to the north-east and east of the enemy battleship. At 9.15pm, Captain Dalrymple-Hamilton of the *Rodney* reversed course, turning to starboard to avoid crossing the flagship's line of fire. Tovey ordered a turn to port, which meant that by 9.20am both *Rodney* and *King George V* had reversed course, and were both on a parallel course to that of the *Bismarck*, with *Rodney* in the lead, followed 6,000 yards (3 miles) astern by the flagship. The turn also meant that both battleships could continue to fire with all their turrets.

The *Bismarck*'s after turret was silenced by 9.25am, leaving just 'Caesar' turret able to fire back, albeit only under local control. A minute later it too was put out of action, leaving the German battleship virtually defenceless. After some frantic damage-control work, 'Anton' turret was back in operation at 9.27am, but managed to fire only one or possibly two salvoes under local control before it too was knocked out just three minutes later.

The pall of smoke in the distance marks the location of the *Bismarck*, in this action photograph taken from the *Dorsetshire* at 10.15am on 27 May. *Rodney* in the foreground was about to cease fire and break off the action.

THE FINAL DESTRUCTION OF THE *BISMARCK*, 9.45AM, 27 MAY 1941 (pp.82–83)

Once two fully operational British battleships overhauled her, the stricken KMS *Bismarck* had little chance of surviving the encounter, both because she was outgunned, and also owing to her lack of manoeuvrability. HMS *Rodney* opened fire at 8.47am, followed a minute later by Vice Admiral Tovey's flagship HMS *King George V*. *Bismarck* returned fire, aiming at *Rodney*. After ten minutes a hit disabled *Bismarck*'s forward gunnery director, which made it far more difficult for her to aim her guns with any real accuracy. Over the next 30 minutes the *Bismarck* was hit repeatedly, losing the use of her after gunnery director, and all of her four turrets **(1)**. She became a blazing wreck, almost incapable of defending herself. The British battleships closed the range, and kept firing.

By 9.40am – almost an hour after the battle began – HMS *Rodney* **(2)** was just 4,000 yards (2 miles) away on Bismarck's port beam, while *King George V* was 6,000 yards (3 miles) away, off her port quarter. Both battleships were now firing with both their main and secondary armament, and at those ranges the majority of their shells hit their target. The *Bismarck* was still floating, as most of the damage was above her waterline, but she was listing slightly to port **(3)** owing to flooding from several waterline hits, and her superstructure forward of her after turrets was ablaze **(4)**. To the observers in the British ships her hull seemed to glow – the result of internal fires. The firing would continue for 30 more minutes, by which time it was clear that the *Bismarck* wouldn't be sunk by gunnery alone. At that point Tovey ordered his two battleships to break off the action, and sent in the cruiser *Dorsetshire* to finish off the *Bismarck* with her torpedoes. She finally sank at 10.40am.

By that time – 9.30am – as well as her main guns being out of action, much of her secondary armament was also silenced by damage to the turrets themselves, or to the secondary gun directors. The *Bismarck* had been battered into submission in just under three-quarters of an hour, and she had become little more than a floating wreck.

Surprisingly, her watertight integrity was still good. Her armour still protected her hull from the worst penetrating hits, but her superstructure was now a battered shambles of wrecked steel, and fires were raging from stem to stern. In other words, the battleships could wreck the *Bismarck*, but they were unable to sink her. Still the shells kept on thudding into her – several hits being scored every minute, from 8in., 14in. and 16in. shells. Tovey was reluctant to cease firing – because fires obscured the British handiwork, he was unsure just how serious the damage to the *Bismarck* actually was. The two battleships edged ever closer, until by 9.40am the *Rodney* lay just 4,000 yards (2 miles) to the north-west of the *Bismarck*, while *King George V* was 6,000 yards (3 miles) to the west. *Norfolk* and *Dorsetshire* prowled 12,000 yards (6 miles) to the east of the stricken battleship.

Tovey was determined to finish the job. He knew that by 10am at the latest his two battleships would have to break off the action, or risk running out of fuel in mid-Atlantic. Even then, he barely had enough fuel reserves left to reach port at half speed. By then it was clear that the *Bismarck* was finished, Her superstructure seemed to glow orange from the fires raging throughout the ship, and in her hull. In fact, the *Bismarck* had suffered several penetrating hits on or below her waterline, causing fires and flooding. Her engines had stopped, and she was now merely wallowing in the swell. All signs of resistance had now ceased. If it weren't for the *Hood*, the British gunners might have felt more sympathy for their German counterparts. Still, the salvoes kept slamming into her.

By 10am it was clear that gunnery alone wasn't going to sink the *Bismarck*. She was now pointing towards the north-west, with *Rodney* on one side and *King George V* on the other. The two British cruisers were also closing the range, and Tovey decided to break off the action, and leave the *Dorsetshire* to finish the *Bismarck* off with her torpedoes. He had left it as long as he could, but at 10.15am he ordered *Rodney* and *King George V* to cease firing and head back towards Scapa Flow, accompanied by *Norfolk*, who had already fired off her torpedoes.

The heavy cruiser HMS *Dorsetshire* was the last British warship to fire on *Bismarck*, as she finished her off with torpedoes, fired from close range at 10.24am and 10.30am. Minutes later the battleship began to settle by the stern.

The final moments of the *Bismarck*, captured from the deck of the British heavy cruiser *Dorsetshire*, which had circled the stricken battleship and fired eight torpedoes at her. These torpedo hits were probably what finally caused the *Bismarck* to sink.

On the *Bismarck*, the order had already been given to abandon ship. The bridge had been hit several times, and by that stage both Admiral Lütjens and Kapitän Lindemann were dead, their bodies buried somewhere in the burning wreckage. Explosive scuttling charges had already been rigged, and the order was given to open the sea valves on the underside of the *Bismarck*'s hull to speed the sinking. Even then, the German fear was that the battered floating wreckage might be captured and towed back to Britain as the ultimate trophy of war. The engineers needn't have bothered. Within minutes the *Dorsetshire* had closed to within 1,000 yards (910m), and was preparing to fire her torpedoes at the floating, blazing maelstrom.

At 10.24am she fired two torpedoes that struck the battleship amidships on her starboard side. *Dorsetshire* then circled the bows of the *Bismarck* to fire two more into her port side six minutes later. We still don't know how many of these torpedoes hit their target, but the result was that while minor explosions rippled through her hull, the *Bismarck* finally began to sink. She settled by her stern, listing slightly to port as she did so. She was still facing towards the north-east. Within a minute the list to port had increased markedly, and she slowly rolled over onto her mangled side.

Pieces of her superstructure began to break away, and her four turrets fell out of their barbettes into the churning sea. After all, only gravity had been holding them in place. Those crewmen who still remained on her blazing upper deck scrambled onto her exposed hull, while others tried desperately to swim to safety, before they were sucked under. Then she slowly rolled over even further, and at 10.40am she slipped gurgling and hissing beneath the waters of the Atlantic Ocean.

The water around her was filled with debris, oil and men, many of them badly burned or injured. *Dorsetshire* edged through the wreckage to pick up survivors, throwing ropes and nets over her side as her crew tried to pull whoever they could to safety. Minutes later the destroyer *Maori* also arrived, and the grim task of recovering the survivors began. Then, the lookout on the *Dorsetshire* spotted a periscope in the water – or at least he thought he did. Captain Martin had no alternative but to get his cruiser under way – the safety of his own ship and men were more important than those poor survivors in the water. *Maori* set off to try and locate the U-boat, and then was ordered to follow *Dorsetshire* as she steamed away to safety. Between them the two British ships had managed to rescue 116 survivors (one of whom died on board *Dorsetshire*). The *Bismarck* carried a crew of just over 2,000 men. While most of these went down with their ship, according to the survivor Müllenheim-Rechberg an estimated 800 men were left behind in the water. Of these, five were still alive the next day when they were rescued by *U-75* and the German weather ship *Sachsenwald*, which had raced to the scene. The rest paid the ultimate price for Germany's brief and spectacular challenge to British seapower.

The final agonies of the *Bismarck*, as depicted in *Sinking of the Bismarck* by Charles E. Turner (1883–1965). As the German battleship heels over to port the heavy cruiser HMS *Dorsetshire* can be seen lying off her port side, about to fire the salvo of torpedoes that finally sent the *Bismarck* to the bottom. Print from Author's Collection.

AFTERMATH

The survivors told their rescuers a harrowing tale. They escaped from a floating hell, where dead seamen or horrifically injured and dying young men lay everywhere. The passageways and decks were covered in blood and gore, and those who made it out had to fight their way past their shipmates who were too badly injured to escape. Many were trapped below decks by hatches that couldn't be opened thanks to shell damage, and the cries of the wounded and dying were heart-rending. Those who made it out onto the upper deck encountered a similar scene, with the added hazard of fires raging out of control.

One of these survivors was Kapitänleutnant von Müllenheim-Rechberg, the only officer to escape from the sinking ship. When his gunnery equipment was wrecked, and the guns silenced, he made his way down to the deck, where he saw just how bad the damage really was. 'Everything up to the bridge bulwarks had been destroyed. The hatches leading to the main deck were jammed shut… flames cut off the whole forward part of the ship. Hundreds of crewmen lay where they had been hit, in the foretop, on the bridge, in the control stations, at the guns, on the upper deck, and on the main and battery decks.' He eventually reached the quarterdeck, where he was able to jump into the sea and swim away from the sinking ship.

Another survivor told how the dead and wounded littered the upper deck, and when the ship began to list many of these men were washed into the sea, where the waves often threw them back against the side of the ship. Others also told of hundreds of men trapped inside the ship by jammed hatches, while others sat around, as if resigned to their fate. Sailors were driven mad, while others took their own lives. All the while more shells were striking the ship, ripping holes in the superstructure or decks, and causing even more chaos, death and horror. Those that made it through the floating hell to the quarterdeck slipped into the water, and tried to escape.

The airmen on a Swordfish from *Ark Royal* flying over the scene described how hundreds of bodies – alive and dead – bobbed around in the water as the ship finally went under. Those were the men who swam towards the *Dorsetshire*, hoping that the worst was behind them. Instead, hundreds were unavoidably left to their fate, as the cruiser was forced to steam away.

On *King George V*, Vice Admiral Tovey witnessed the dying minutes of the *Bismarck*, and he later paid a moving testimony to her men. 'The *Bismarck* had put up a most gallant fight against impossible odds, worthy of the old days of the Imperial German Navy, and she went down with her colours flying.' It was a spectacular and Wagnerian end to a worthy foe.

HMS *Prince of Wales*, photographed at Scapa Flow before her encounter with the *Bismarck* in the Denmark Strait. Her new paint betrays the fact that she was fresh from the shipyard, and she was still plagued by mechanical 'teething troubles'.

Of course, the campaign didn't end suddenly with the sinking of the *Bismarck*. Like any naval campaign, there were loose ends. One of these was the *Prinz Eugen*, which parted company with the *Bismarck* on the evening of 24 May. She steamed south towards the main transatlantic convoy routes, and away from the British warships searching for the *Bismarck*. Two days later she rendezvoused with the German tanker *Spichern*, and refuelled in mid-Atlantic. Kapitän Brinkmann still planned to hunt for British convoys, but he spent three fruitless days searching for them. In fact, the Admiralty had diverted them away from the area, fearing they might inadvertently run into either the *Bismarck* or her former consort.

Then, on 29 May, a fault developed with her engines, and Brinkmann decided to head back to port, and turned towards the French coast. That was two days after the sinking of the *Bismarck*, and the Home Fleet had already returned to Scapa Flow or other British ports. This meant that the Western Approaches were relatively free of British warships, and the *Prinz Eugen* finally reached the safety of Brest on 1 June. Less fortunate were the German tankers and supply ships, scattered throughout the Atlantic to support the *Bismarck*. They were all located and destroyed in the weeks that followed.

In February 1942 the *Prinz Eugen* slipped out of port in company with the battlecruisers *Scharnhorst* and *Gneisenau*, and headed through the English Channel to reach the safety of German and Norwegian ports. The 'Channel Dash' was a daring and successful enterprise, but it revealed that the Kriegsmarine were no longer interested in using their vulnerable surface ships to attack the Atlantic convoys. After the loss of the *Bismarck*, the Seekriegsleitung was extremely unwilling to risk their remaining capital ships in what they saw as a suicidal venture.

As for the British ships that took part in the pursuit of the *Bismarck*, several would succumb to enemy action before the end of the war. The Tribal-

class destroyer *Mashona* was sunk by prowling German bombers the day after the *Bismarck*, as she headed home through the Western Approaches. On 13 November the *Ark Royal* was torpedoed by a German U-boat as she returned to her base at Gibraltar after a foray into the Mediterranean. The *Prince of Wales* was repaired after the damage she suffered at the hands of the *Bismarck*, and she was then sent to the Far East. On 10 December 1941 Japanese aircraft off the coast of Malaya sank her and the battlecruiser *Repulse*. However significant these British losses might have been, they never altered the naval balance in favour of the Axis powers, while the loss of the *Bismarck* had a significant impact on German naval power, and an equally dramatic influence on the Kriegsmarine's belief in its own abilities.

The heavy cruiser *Prinz Eugen*, photographed after her safe arrival in Brest on 1 June 1941. Kapitän Brinkmann managed to evade the British, and had sailed 7,000 miles (13,000km) since leaving Gotenhafen two weeks earlier, thereby bringing Operation *Rheinübung* to a close.

Of course, both sides could argue that they made mistakes during the campaign. If the *Bismarck* had refuelled in Norway it might have been able to reach Brest at full speed, even after suffering damage during the battle of the Denmark Strait. During the battle, Holland might have handled his ships better, and reduced the risk to his vulnerable flagship. Similarly, if Lütjens had not been constrained by orders, he might have been able to finish off the *Prince of Wales*, rather than break off the action. Then there was Lütjens' signal, which told the British roughly where to look. If any of these mistakes had been avoided, Operation *Rheinübung* might have ended very differently.

The 'what if' aspects of the campaign are certainly fascinating, especially as the *Bismarck* came so close to evading her pursuers. As Winston Churchill put it: 'Had she escaped, the moral effects of her continuing existence, as much as the material damage she might have inflicted on our shipping, would have been calamitous. Many misgivings would have arisen regarding our capacity to control the oceans, and these would have been trumpeted around the world, to our great detriment and discomfort.' Fortunately for Great Britain, the sortie proved a disaster for the Kriegsmarine, and the Royal Navy remained the unchallenged arbiters of seapower. As Großadmiral Raeder admitted; 'The loss of the *Bismarck* had a decisive effect on the conduct of the war at sea.' With hindsight, it is easy to assume that the *Bismarck* was doomed from the moment she set sail. During that long tense week in May 1941, the situation was a lot less clear cut.

THE SHIPWRECK

As the *Bismarck* sank her funnel, what was left of her masts and her four gun turrets all broke away, and made their own way to the seabed, 5,000 yards (4,572m) below the surface of the Atlantic. The ship itself was facing towards the north-west, and lying on her port side shortly before she finally sank, and, although she rolled over further as she began sinking by the stern, she righted herself as she went down. The British placed the position of her sinking at 48°10' North, and 16°12' West, but this was based on dead reckoning, as the skies were too overcast to permit an accurate navigational fix using the sun or stars. After she submerged *Bismarck* also glided some distance as she sank, unlike the turrets, which virtually fell vertically towards the ocean floor. As a result, the location of her resting place was known only very approximately.

In July 1988, after his successful location of the RMS *Titanic*, the deep-sea explorer and scientist Dr Robert Ballard began searching for the wreck of the *Bismarck*. He began by searching the location given by the Royal Navy, but he found nothing. He returned and widened the search, covering over 200 square miles (520 square kilometres) of seabed before he finally located the shipwreck on 8 June 1989. She actually lay some distance from the given position – the result of her underwater glide as much as the lack of precise wartime navigation. It also appears that when she hit the seabed she continued moving for another 3,000ft (910m), leaving a trail of debris as she went, before finally coming to rest in 15,700ft (4,790m) of water.

Before Ballard and his team discovered her she had lain there undisturbed for almost half a century, her jagged scars softened by marine growth, and her broken hull a haven for marine life. The team explored the ship herself and the debris field behind her, in an attempt to piece together her final moments, and to understand the full extent of the damage inflicted on her during her last battle. The *Bismarck* is resting upright on the seabed, embedded in mud as far as her waterline. She carries the scars of the dreadful pounding she received on the morning of 27 May, but otherwise her hull is remarkably intact, missing only the last 10m (30ft) of her stern, which broke away during her sinking.

Ballard followed the debris trail backwards to discover her turrets, lying upside down on the seabed, marking the spot where the *Bismarck* actually sank. The debris trail itself is littered with broken pieces of superstructure, such as her funnel, her masts and her gun directors. On the ship itself the torn teak decking can still be seen on the quarterdeck, where Müllenheim-Rechberg jumped into the sea, and the mangled remains of the bridge can still be seen, where Admiral Lütjens and Kapitän Lindemann went down with their ship.

In July 2001 a deep-sea exploration team led by David L. Mearns also located the wreck of the battlecruiser *Hood*, her shattered remains lying 9,000ft (2,800m) below the surface of the Denmark Strait. The examination helped to explain why she blew up so quickly, and showed just how cataclysmic the explosion was which tore her apart. Both exploration teams treated the shipwrecks they found as if they were war graves, and went to great lengths to avoid disturbing the final resting places of so many sailors. Plaques were laid next to the wreck sites, honouring the 3,500 men who lost their lives when the two ships sank. Once the exploration teams departed, the two mighty protagonists were once again left in peace in the cold and darkness of the Atlantic floor.

BIBLIOGRAPHY

Bekker, Cajus, *Hitler's Naval War* Macdonald and Jane's: London, 1974

Berthold, Will, *Sink the Bismarck* Longmans: London, 1968

Bradford, Ernle, *The Mighty Hood* Hodder & Stoughton: London, 1959

Brennecke, Jochen, *Schlachtshiffe Bismarck* Naval Institute Press: Annapolis, MD, 1960

Busch, Fritz-Otto, *The Story of the Prinz Eugen* Hale: New York, 1960

Chesneau, Roger, *Hood: Life and death of a Battlecruiser* Cassell: London, 2002

Dönitz, Grand Admiral Karl, *Memoirs: Ten Years and Twenty Days* Weidenfeld and Nicholson: London, 1958

Forester, C. S., *Hunting the Bismarck* Granada Publishing: London, 1963

Herwig, Holger H., and Bercuson, David J., *The Destruction of the Bismarck* Overlook Press: Overlook, NY, 2001

Humble, Richard, *Hitler's High Seas Fleet* Ballantine: New York, 1971

Jackson, Robert, *The Bismarck* Spellmount: Staplehurst, 2002

Kennedy, Ludovic, *Pursuit: The Chase and sinking of the Bismarck* William Collins Sons & Co.: London, 1974

Konstam, Angus, *Hunt the Bismarck* Naval Institute Press: Annapolis, MD, 2003

Mearns, David, and White, Rob, *Hood and Bismarck: The Deep-Sea Discovery of an epic battle* Channel 4 Books: London, 2001

Müllenheim-Rechberg, Baron Burkhard von, *Battleship Bismarck: A Survivor's Story* Naval Institute Press: Annapolis, MD, 1990

Rhys-Jones, Graham, *The Loss of the Bismarck: An Avoidable Disaster* Naval Institute Press: Annapolis, MD, 2000

Schmalenbach, Paul, *KM Bismarck* Profile Publications: Windsor, 1972

Shirer, W. L., *All about the sinking of the Bismarck* W. H. Allen Publishing: London, 1963

Stephen, Martin, *Sea Battles in Close-Up: World War 2* Ian Allen: London, 1988

Vian, Admiral of the Fleet Sir Philip, *Action this Day* Frederick Muller Press: London, 1960

Whitley, M. J., *Cruisers of World War Two: An International Encyclopedia* Brockhampton Press: London, 1995

Whitley, M. J., *Battleships of World War Two: An International Encyclopedia* Arms & Armour Press: London, 1998

Winklareth, Robert J., *The Bismarck Chase: New Light on a Famous Engagement* Chatham Publishing: London, 1998

INDEX

Figures in bold refere to images.

Achates, HMS 33
aircraft (British)
    Beaufort torpedo bombers 14
    Catalina flying boats 59, 64
    Hurricane fighters 22
    Swordfish torpedo bombers 22, 57,
      58–59, 60, 61, *61*, 65, 65–74, 68,
      69, 70–71 (72)
Antelope, HMS 33
Anthony, HMS 33
Arethusa, HMS 33, 36, 56–57
Ark Royal, HMS 19, 22, 57, *60*, *61*, 65,
    70 – 71 (72), 91
Aurora, HMS 37, 58

Ballard, Dr Robert 92
Beaufort torpedo bombers 14
Birmingham, HMS 33, 36, 56–57
Bismarck, KMS *7*, *10*, *11*, 13, *13*
    aftermath 88–91
    Battle of the Denmark Strait 39–53,
      40, 42, 46–47 (48), 50, 53
    the breakout 30–39
    camouflage 5, 23, 31, 35
    chronology 8–9
    design and development 22–25
    the last battle 77–87, 80, 82–83
      (84), 86, 87
    Operation *Rheinübung* (1941) 30,
      30–87, 33
    plans for the campaign 27–29, 28
    pursuit of 53–76, 57, 73
    the shipwreck 92–93
    specifications 25
Bovell, Captain 58
Brest, France 11, 12, 13, 14, 54
Briggs, Flying Officer *59*
Brinkmann, Kapitän zur See Helmuth
    18, *18*, 31, 49, 58, 90
Britain, Battle of (1940) 5
British ships
    Achates 33
    Antelope 33
    Anthony 33
    Arethusa 33, 36, 56–57
    Ark Royal 19, 22, 57, 60, 61, 65,
      70–71 (72), 91
    Birmingham 33, 36, 56–57
    Colossus 15
    Cossack 20, 75
    Dorsetshire 20, 25, 63, 81, 82–83
      (84), 85, 86, 87, *87*, 88
    Echo 33
    Electra 33, 54
    Galatea 37, 58
    Hermione 37
    Hood 6, 12, 16, 19, 21–22, 25, 27, 33,
      36, 37, 39–51, 40, 41, 42, 49, 51, 93

Icarus 33
Kenya 37, 58
King George V 19, *19*, 20, 25, 27,
    31, 33, 36, 37, 49, 58, 59, 61, 62,
    77, 80–81, 82–83 (84), 85
Manchester 33, 36, 56–57
Maori 20, 75, *75*, 87
Mashona 57, 91
Neptune 37, 58
Norfolk 19, 21, 25, 26, 33, 35–36,
    39, 58, 62, 77, 80, 81, 85
Onslow 15
Prince of Wales 18, 19, 20–21, 25,
    27, 33, 36, 39–52, 49, 51, 52, 54,
    58, 60, 62, 90, 91
Ramillies 19, 21, 57, 63
Renown 18, 19, 21, 27, 57, 60, 65, 77
Repulse 19, 21, 33, 36, 37, 54,
    58, 59, 61, 62, 91
Revenge 19, 57
Rodney 15, 19, 20, 21, 25, 56–57,
    63, 76, 77, *77*, 80–81, 81, 82–83
    (84), 85
Sheffield 19, 57, 64, 65, 69, 74
Sikh 20, 75
Somali 57
Suffolk 19, 25, 26, 27, 33, 35–36, 39,
    40, 40, 58, 60, 62
Tartar 57
Victorious 19, 22, 27, 33, 54, 56,
    57, 58, 61
Zulu 20

camouflage *5, 23*, 31, *35*
Cape Matapan 10
Cape Spartivento, Battle of (1940) 16
Carls, Generaladmiral Rolf 17
Catalina flying boats *59*, 64
Cherbourg, France 11
'Channel Dash,' the 90
chronology 8–9
Churchill, Prime Minister Sir Winston
    10, 15, *15*, 91
Colossus, HMS 15
commanders
    British 15–17
    German 17–18
'commerce warfare' 11
convoys, Allied 12, 14, 15
Cossack, HMS 20, 75
Crete, evacuation of (1941) 10–11
Curteis, Rear Admiral 58

Dalrymple-Hamilton, Captain 63, 81
Denham, Captain Henry *31*
Denmark Strait, Battle of (1941) 18,
    39–53
Dönitz, Admiral 24
Dorsetshire, HMS 20, 25, 63, 81,
    82 – 83 (84), *85*, 86, 87, *87, 88*

Echo, HMS 33
Electra, HMS 33, 54
Ellis, Captain 39, 61
Esmonde, Lieutenant-Commander
    58–59
Eugene of Savoy 23

Faeroe Islands 34
Force H (British) 19, 21, 57, 59, *60*,
    64, 65
France, invasion of (1940) 10
Fricke, Admiral Kurt 17

Galatea, HMS 37, 58
German Navy see Kriegsmarine
German ships *see also Bismarck*, KMS
    Gneisenau 13, 14, 18, 28, 90
    Graf Spee 11, 29
    Karlsrühe 18
    Prinz Eugen 5, 13, *13*, 14, 18, 23–24,
      24, 25, 28, 30, 31, 33, 34, 36, 39,
      41, 44–45, 49, 52, 53–54, 61, 91
    Sachsenwald 87
    Scharnhorst 12, 13, 14, 18, 54, 90
    Spichern (tanker) 90
    Tirpitz 14
    Weissenburg (tanker) 34
    Wiesbaden 15
    Wollin (tanker) 31
Gneisenau, KMS 12, 13, 14, 18, 28, 90
Godfrey-Faussett, Lieutenant *70 – 71*
    (72)
Gotland (Sweden) 31
Graf Spee, KMS 11, 29
Great Belt, the 30
Greece, evacuation of (1941) 10
Grimstadfjord, Norway 31

Hermione, HMS 37
Hipper, Admiral 17
Hitler, Adolf *13*, 23
Holland, Vice Admiral Lancelot 16, *16*,
    33, 36, 91
    Battle of the Denmark Strait 40, 41,
      42–50, 51
Home Fleet (British) 10–11, 13, 15,
    15, 20, 21, 36, 37, 41, *54*, 59,
    64, 90
Hood, HMS *6, 12*, 16, 19, 21–22,
    27, 93
    Battle of the Denmark Strait (1941)
      39–51, 40, 41, 42, 49, 51
    the breakout 33, 36, 37
    specifications 25
Hurricane fighters 22

Icarus, HMS 33
Iceland 27, 33, 34–35

Jutland, Battle of (1916) 12, 15, 17

Karlsrühe, SMS 18
Kattegat, the 31
Kenya, HMS 37, 58
Kerr, Captain 41, 43, 45, 51
King George V, HMS 19, *19*, 20, 27
  Battle of the Denmark Strait 49
  the breakout 31, 33, 36, 37
  the last battle 77, 80–81, 82–83
    (84), 85
  pursuit of the *Bismarck* 58, 59,
    61, 62
  specifications 25
Kriegsmarine see also German ships
  aftermath 88–91
  Battle of the Denmark Strait 39–53
  the breakout 30–39
  chronology 8–9
  commanders 17–18
  the fleet 22–25
  the last battle 77–87
  North Atlantic 1941, map of 4
  Operation *Berlin* (1941) 12, 18
  Operation *Rheinübung* (1941) 6–7,
    13–14, 30–87
  origins of the campaign 10–14
  plans for the campaign 27–29
  and the pursuit of the *Bismarck*
    53–76
  U-boats 5, 11, 17, 24, 58, 87

Leach, Captain 21, 44, 45, 51, 52–53,
  56, 58, 61
Lindemann, Kapitän zur See Ernst *17*,
  18, 23, 39, 52, 53, 73, 74, 80, 86
Luftwaffe 11, 69
Lütjens, Admiral Günther 13, 14, *17*,
  18, 31, 34, 37, 91
  Battle of the Denmark Strait 39, 40,
    41, 42–43, 44–45, 49
  the last battle 80, 86
  Operation *Berlin* (1941) 12
  opposing plans 27–29
  the pursuit of the *Bismarck* 53–54,
    58, 60–62, 64–65, 76

Modoc (US Coastguard Ship) 58
Manchester, HMS 33, 36, 56–57
Maori, HMS 20, 75, *75*, 87
Marlborough, Duke of 23
Martin, Captain 87
Mashona, HMS 57, 91
Mearns, David L. 93
Mers-el-Kebir, Algeria 16–17
minesweepers 31
Moffat, Sub-Lieutenant *70 – 71* (72)
Müllenheim-Rechberg, Kapitänleutnant
  von 88

Neptune, HMS 37, 58
Norfolk, HMS 19, *21*, 25, *26*,
  33, 35–36, 39, 58, 62, 77, 80,
  81, 85

Norway, invasion of (1940) 11

Onslow, HMS 15
Operation *Berlin* (1941) 12, 18
Operation *Rheinübung* (1941) 6–7,
  13–14, 30–87
Owen-Smith, Lieutenant *70 – 71* (72)

Phillips, Captain 39
'phoney war' 10
Piorun (Polish) 20, 75, 77
Pound, Admiral Sir Dudley 15
Prince of Wales, HMS 18, 19, 20–21, 27
  aftermath 90, 91
  Battle of the Denmark Strait 39–52,
    49, 51, 52
  the breakout 33, 36
  pursuit of the *Bismarck* 54, 58,
    60, 62
  specifications 25
Prinz Eugen, KMS *5*, 13, *13*, 14,
  18, 28
  aftermath 90, 91
  Battle of the Denmark Strait 41,
    44–45, 49
  the breakout 30, 31, 33, 34, 36, 39
  design and development 23–24, *24*
  and the pursuit of the *Bismarck*
    52, 53–54, 61
  specifications 25

radar 39, 40, 58
Raeder, Großadmiral Erich 11, 12–13,
  14, 17, 29, 34, 91
Ramillies, HMS 19, 21, 57, 63
Renown, HMS 18, 19, 21, 27, 57, *60*,
  65, 77
Repulse, HMS 19, 21, 33, 36, 37, *54*,
  58, 59, 61, 62, 91
Revenge, HMS 19, 57
Rodney, HMS 15, 19, *20*, 21
  the last battle 77, *77*, 80–81, *81*,
    82–83 (84), 85
  the pursuit of the *Bismarck* 56–57,
    63, 76
  specifications 25
Royal Air Force (RAF) 14, 22, 36
Royal Navy 6–7 see also British ships
  aftermath 88–91
  Battle of the Denmark Strait 39–53
  the breakout 30–39
  chronology 8–9
  commanders 15–17
  evacuation of Crete (1941) 10–11
  the fleet 19–22, 25
  the last battle 77–87
  and Operation *Rheinübung* (1941)
    30–87
  plans for the campaign 26–27
  pursuit of the *Bismarck* 53–76

Saalwächter, Generaladmiral Alfred 17

Sachsenwald, KMS 87
Saint-Nazaire, France 11, 54
Scapa Flow 6, *12*, 15, *15*, 17, 19, 36, 37,
  41, 90, *90*
Scharnhorst, KMS 12, 13, 14, 18,
  54, 90
Schmundt, Vizeadmiral Hubert 17
Schniewind, Generaladmiral Otto 12,
  13, 14, 17, 27–29, 34
Sheffield, HMS 19, 57, *64*, 65, 69,
  74
Sikh, HMS 20, 75
Somali, HMS 57
Somerville, Vice Admiral Sir James *16*,
  16–17, 57, 59, *60*, 65, 77
specifications, ships 25
Spichern (German tanker) 90
Suckling, Flying Officer 31
Suffolk, HMS 19, 25, *26*, *27*,
  33, 35–36, 39, 40, *40*, 58,
  60, 62
Sweden 31
Swordfish torpedo bombers 22,
  57, 58–59, *60*, 61, *61*, 65,
  65–74, *68*, *69*, *70 – 71*
  (72)

tankers, German 24, 90
Taranto 10
Tartar, HMS 57
Tirpitz, KMS 14
Tovey, Vice Admiral Sir John 6, *15*,
  15–16
  aftermath 88
  the breakout 31, 33, 36–39
  the British fleet 19, 21, 22
  the last battle 77, 85
  plans for the campaign 26–27
  pursuit of the *Bismarck* 58, 61,
    62–65, 74–75
Trondheim, Norway 34

U-boats 5, 11, 17, 24, 58, 87

Versailles Treaty (1919) 22, 23
Vian, Captain Philip 65, *74*, 75
Victorious, HMS 19, 22, 27, 33, *54*,
  56, *57*, 58, 61

Wake-Walker, Rear Admiral William *16*,
  17, *21*, *26*
  Battle of Denmark Strait 40, 51
  the breakout 33, 35–36, 39
  the last battle 77
  pursuit of the *Bismarck* 54, 56, 58,
    60, 62
Washington Naval Treaty (1922) *20*
Weissenburg (German tanker) 34
Wiesbaden, SMS 15
Wollin (German tanker) 31

Zulu, HMS 20, 75